■ SCHOLASTI

READ & RESPOND

Bringing the best books to life in the classroom

Guided Reading

Key Stage 2

Comprehensive guided reading notes for:

- **Bill's New Frock**
- **The Owl Who Was Afraid of the Dark**
- **The Twits**
- **The Iron Man**
- **Diary of a Wimpy Kid**
- **Danny the Champion of the World**

AGES
7–8

Scholastic Education, an imprint of Scholastic Ltd
Book End, Range Road, Witney, Oxfordshire, OX29 0YD
Registered office: Westfield Road, Southam, Warwickshire CV47 0RA
www.scholastic.co.uk
© 2017, Scholastic Ltd
1 2 3 4 5 6 7 8 9   7 8 9 0 1 2 3 4 5 6

British Library Cataloguing-in-Publication Data
A catalogue record for this book is available from the British Library.
ISBN 978-1407-16947-7
Printed and bound by Ashford Colour Press

Due to the nature of the web we cannot guarantee the content or links of any site mentioned. We strongly recommend that teachers check websites before using them in the classroom.

Every effort has been made to trace copyright holders for the works reproduced in this book, and the publishers apologise for any inadvertent omissions.

Extracts from National Curriculum for England, English Programme of Study © Crown Copyright. Reproduced under the terms of the Open Government Licence (OGL). www.nationalarchives.gov.uk/doc/open-government-licence/version/3/

Authors Sally Burt, Pam Dowson, Samantha Pope, Debbie Ridgard, Sarah Snashall
Editorial Rachel Morgan, Jenny Wilcox, Kate Buckley, Emily Anderson, Marion Archer
Cover and Series Design Neil Salt and Nicolle Thomas
Layout Neil Salt

CONTENTS ▼

▼ INTRODUCTION

Read & Respond provides teaching ideas related to a specific children's book. The series focuses on best-loved books and brings you ways to use them to engage your class and enthuse them about reading. This book provides detailed guided reading sessions for six children's books.

GUIDED READING

Guided reading is usually conducted in small groups with children of a similar reading ability, under teacher guidance. The groups are often around six to eight children, although may be fewer depending on the children in your class. The sessions are likely to be short, around 20 minutes, and focused on reading and comprehension skills.

There should be one focus text and each child should have a copy of it. The text should be slightly more challenging than the children's independent reading level, where they can read and understand the vast majority of the text independently. The teacher facilitation of guided reading allows for the children to access more challenging materials in a supported environment – they should still be able to understand and access 90 per cent of the content though.

Guided reading is much more than just reading in turns. Time should be given for reading independently; the teacher may wish to listen to individual children, but this should be followed up by checking the children's understanding and comprehension of the text through discussion and questioning.

How this book relates to the *Read & Respond* teacher's book

This book can be used for stand-alone sessions or in conjunction with the corresponding *Read & Respond* teacher's books. Each *Read & Respond* teacher's book is designed for whole-class teaching and contains a variety of activities that look at grammar, punctuation and spelling; plot, character and setting; speaking and listening; and writing.

While there are guided reading notes in the teacher's book, the ones provided in this book are much more detailed and therefore the two books can work together. If you are using a carousel system for guided reading, then the teacher's book may provide supporting activities to use when the children are not in the guided reading group. Within this book, there may be some optional links referenced to the *Read & Respond* teacher's book, where work could be expanded.

ABOUT THE BOOK

Each children's book has been divided into six guided reading sessions. The sessions work through each book progressively, so you read it over a number of weeks. It has been assumed that the sessions will be conducted in guided reading groups of around six to eight children; if you plan to use them differently, then they can be adapted accordingly. Each session follows a similar structure:

Session aims: The purpose of the session and what children will be focused on in their reading.

Before the session: If there is anything the children need to do prior to the session, such as reading some of the book, this will be identified here.

Read: This section will focus on the children reading the text either independently or as a group. It may be reading new chapters or sections of the book or re-reading parts of the book that they have read previously. They should consider questions about the text while reading and then discuss these as a group to check their understanding.

Revisit and respond: A range of different activities will have been provided under this heading to provide flexibility to select appropriate tasks for the group. As each session is only intended to be around 20 minutes long, it is advised that one or two of these activity ideas are used to meet the needs of your children.

Assessment opportunities: A bank of questions has been provided which could be used at any point in the session as relevant. They are sub-divided into headings to identify the purpose of the type of question.

At the end of the book, you will find two templates that you can use to support your guided reading sessions:

Guided Reading Bookmark Template: This template provides a bookmark that you can complete and give to the children as reference. It could include the questions you want them to consider when reading or you could use the assessment opportunities questions for the children to discuss.

Guided Reading Record Template: A template to record any notes from a guided reading session so you have a record that you can refer to.

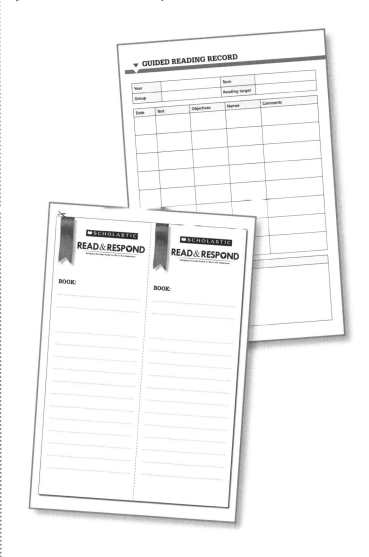

SESSION AIMS

Learn about Bill's dilemma and identify stereotypical behaviour towards boys and girls.

READ

- Look together at the cover of the book. Ask: *What is unexpected about the title? What might the story be about?* Note that the book won the Smarties Prize, suggesting it is well thought of. Do the children know any other books by Anne Fine? (Some are listed on the inside pages of the book.)

- Ask the children to read the first page silently to themselves. Ask for their reactions. Invite them to look at the illustration of Bill looking in the mirror – can they see any evidence in the picture that Bill is a boy?

- Ask the children to read up to the end of the handwriting lesson, ending with 'stop himself from thumping Philip'.

During reading

- Ask them to make a note of any language that is particularly 'girlish' in nature, and to look for examples of how Bill is treated now that he seems to be a girl.

- When they have finished reading, invite the children to share their observations – for example, they may have found words such as 'dear', 'poppet', 'sweet', 'pretty', and have noted how characters such as Mean Malcolm, the old lady and the teachers behave towards Bill.

- If your school uses reading journals then the children should be encouraged to make notes as they read and consider each question.

- Move around the group and 'tune in' to hear individuals read aloud. Encourage and praise good expression.

REVISIT AND RESPOND

Use the following discussion points to help the children think about what they have read in more depth.

Note: Since there are only 20 minutes for each session, you are advised to focus on only one or two of the elements that are listed below.

- The pace is really fast at the start of the chapter: Mum and Dad are in a hurry and things are happening to Bill in a rush. Ask the children to find examples of words in the text that help to emphasise the speedy pace ('swept', 'rushing', 'ran', 'quickly').

- The author is really trying to make us think about *why* girls and boys are treated differently and how children and adults are both guilty of this behaviour. Ask the children to skim and scan to collect examples that show the ways in which girls are treated that boys would never be (wanting them to be sweet and pretty, whistling at them in the street, suggesting that only boys can carry tables). Encourage the children to discuss this and think of other examples.

- Consider Bill's feelings about the way he is suddenly treated (look for evidence in the text). Does he feel foolish, angry, embarrassed, frustrated?

- We are told Mean Malcolm wears a 'purple studded jacket'. How does this suggest his character? Can the children see a link between this and Bill wearing a dress?

- What do the children think about Astrid's complaint that boys are always chosen instead of girls to move the tables?

- In the handwriting lesson, Bill finds himself writing more neatly than usual, and yet his teacher expects him to be even neater, unlike her expectations of Philip. Ask: *What does this show about some adults' expectations of girls and boys? Is it fair?*

- What is the children's opinion of Philip's remark that 'girls are neater'?

Ask the children, whenever appropriate, to revisit the text to exemplify/support their answers.

Encourage the children to read aloud to the group when referring back to the text – praise clear, confident and expressive reading.

Before the next session
Ask the children to finish reading Chapter 1, thinking about whether Anne Fine is making a serious point about stereotyping boys and girls, or if she is just being light-hearted and funny.

ASSESSMENT OPPORTUNITIES
The following bank of question prompts provides a quick and easy means of monitoring the children's comprehension skills and understanding of the text. The children's answers to a question must be supported by evidence from the text.

Understanding
- What does Bill find when he wakes up on Monday morning?
- What might Bill be thinking when he wakes up to discover he is a girl?
- Describe Bill's new frock.
- Who noticed that he had changed into a girl?
- What happens when Bill meets Mean Malcolm?
- How did the headteacher speak to Bill at the school gates that was different to the way in which he spoke to the other boys arriving?
- Why were all the children keen to be chosen to carry tables to the nursery?
- How do we know that there is no school uniform at Bill's school?
- What differences are there between Bill's and Philip's writing? How did their teacher react to this?
- Do you feel sorry for Bill in the story? Explain why.

Inferences
- How do you think Bill is feeling as he prepares for school that morning? Explain your reasons.
- List the ways that you think Bill's parents might be treating him differently from how they usually do.

- Is Bill embarrassed by being whistled at? Why do you say that?
- Explain why you think the old lady wants to help Bill cross the road.
- Does Bill find there are advantages to being a girl? How do you know that?

Predicting
- Do you think anyone will finally notice that the person in the dress is Bill? What might happen if they do?

Main ideas
- List the ways in which Bill is treated differently because of wearing a dress and seeming to be a girl.

Language, structure and presentation
- Explain why Bill is 'baffled' as he looks in the mirror.
- What does the author mean when she says 'it could be a nightmare'?
- Why do you think Malcolm is known as 'Mean Malcolm'?
- The text states that 'Bill glowered all through the rest of assembly.' Suggest another word that means the same as 'glowered' here.
- How do the occasional illustrations add to the story? Would it be as effective without them?

Themes and conventions
- Give some examples from the story that show how boys and girls are treated differently.

SESSION 2: THE WUMPY CHOO

SESSION AIMS

Use prior knowledge and experience to identify more closely with Bill's point of view.

BEFORE THE SESSION

The children should have read to the end of Chapter 1. They should have with them notes made since the previous session.

READ

- Refer the children to the last incident in Chapter 1, where Bill is asked to read the part of Rapunzel. Ask: *Why do you think the teacher was annoyed when Bill asked her why Rapunzel didn't try to escape from the tower?*

- Ask the children about Bill's suggestion that Rapunzel could have cut off her hair to make a rope to escape. Do they think this is a typical boy's idea or not? Suggest that Anne Fine may have chosen this story and Bill's response in order to extend the idea of stereotyping. Do they agree?

- Invite them to comment on whether they think Anne Fine is making a serious point or simply writing a funny story.

- Ask the children to read Chapter 2 independently, but, before they start, ask if anyone has any ideas about the title – 'The wumpy choo'. Can anyone suggest what a 'wumpy choo' might be?

During reading

- Ask the children to think about how the school playground in the story seems to be divided up between boys and girls, and why this might be. Who seems to be in charge?

- If your school uses reading journals then the children should be encouraged to make notes as they read and consider each question.

- Move around the group and 'tune in' to hear individuals read aloud. Encourage and praise good expression.

REVISIT AND RESPOND

Use the following discussion points to help the children think about what they have read in more depth.

Note: Since there are only 20 minutes for each session, you are advised to focus on only one or two of the elements that are listed below.

- Did any of the children work out what the 'wumpy choo' was before the end of the chapter? Did they enjoy the joke and the play on words? Discuss the difficulty of interpreting words you hear when learning a second language. Do any of the children have any experience of mishearing words, perhaps in song lyrics?

- Ask: *Do you think the girls feel threatened by the boys in the playground? Why, or why not?*

- What is the children's opinion about the boys welcoming other boys into their game but saying that girls get in the way?

- Do boys and girls play separately in your playground? Who decides on what happens and where?

- Look at the illustration of Bill holding the football, surrounded by boys. Ask the children to discuss what is happening here and what the different characters are feeling.

- Does Bill think the boys are fair to the girls? Encourage the children to find evidence in the text. Think about the day before: did Bill think that boys were fair to girls when he was a boy? Ask the children to skim and scan for clues. (Bill seems genuinely shocked at the ways the boys behave, whereas he didn't have to think about it before.)

- Why do the girls in the story allow the boys to behave like this? Invite the children to suggest what the girls could or should do about it. What could or should the teachers do?

- Ask: *What words could you use to describe Bill's actions in arguing with the group of boys?* (Brave, confident, fearless.)

- The chapter provides another example of a difference between boys and girls. This time it seems to be self-imposed – no adults are around during this incident. Invite the children to discuss their own expectations of boys and girls.

- Scan the chapter for words written in italics. Ask: *Why has the author chosen to write these words in italics?* Agree they are being used for emphasis, as an aid to our reading and understanding.

- Bill doesn't know what a 'wumpy choo' is. Why do you think he doesn't ask? (All the girls know and he's uncertain about the rules of being a girl.) Would he have been interested in taking the bet anyway?

Ask the children, whenever appropriate, to revisit the text to exemplify/support their answers.

Encourage the children to read aloud to the group when referring back to the text – praise clear, confident and expressive reading.

Before the next session
Ask the children to read Chapter 3, about the art class, and take note of how the dialogue is presented and how the use of details affects the pace of the narrative.

ASSESSMENT OPPORTUNITIES

The following bank of question prompts provides a quick and easy means of monitoring the children's comprehension skills and understanding of the text. The children's answers to a question must be supported by evidence from the text.

Understanding
- Why does Bill decide to join the girls at playtime?
- What is the bet that Bill takes on?
- Why does Bill agree to take on the bet?
- How do the boys and the girls spend their time at playtime?
- What did Bill think a 'wumpy choo' might be?
- What is a 'wumpy choo'?

Inferences
- Why does Bill feel like crying as he walks away at the end of playtime?
- Who is in charge of what happens in the playground at playtime? How do you know?

- How do we know that Bill begins to realise that the girls are not getting a fair deal at playtime?

Predicting
- After his experiences on the playground, do you think Bill will begin to change in his attitude towards girls? Why do you think that?

Main ideas
- What examples are there in Chapter 2 that show both boys and girls seem to have clear ideas about how they and each other should behave?

Language, structure and presentation
- Explain how the author guides us to read some words in a particular way.
- 'A wumpy choo? Bill Simpson was mystified.' Suggest another word for 'mystified'.

SESSION 3: NO POCKETS

SESSION AIMS

Empathise with the main character through understanding his dilemmas and difficulties.

BEFORE THE SESSION

The children should have read Chapter 3.

READ

- Ask the children to recall the events of Chapter 3, about the pink paint and the art class.
- Invite them to select sections of dialogue that they thought worked particularly well and to read these out to the group.
- Refer the children to the section starting 'A huge glob of pink paint' up to 'What next?'. Draw attention to the use of detail here. Ask: *Why is this effective?* Agree that it slows down the action so that we are almost able to watch the paint spilling down Bill's dress in slow motion, giving us more idea of how Bill and the others feel.
- We read that 'Meekly, he allowed himself to be led to the middle of the room'. Can the children explain the word 'meekly'? Visualise Bill being meekly led. Ask the children to think of other adverbs to replace meekly (such as reluctantly, miserably, sulkily, crossly). Encourage them to visualise Bill each time a new adverb is suggested.
- Ask: *How do you think Bill felt at being chosen as the model in the art class?*
- Explain why Bill compares himself to Rapunzel.
- Continue the session by asking the children to read Chapter 4 independently and then discuss the following points.

During reading
- Think about the further problems that wearing the frock causes for Bill.
- Look out for an example where Anne Fine has again used the device of including detail to slow down an incident that actually happens very quickly (such as when she describes Bill dropping the things he takes to the office).

- If your school uses reading journals then the children should be encouraged to make notes as they read and consider each question.
- Move around the group and 'tune in' to hear individuals read aloud. Encourage and praise good expression.

REVISIT AND RESPOND

Use the following discussion points to help the children think about what they have read in more depth.

Note: Since there are only 20 minutes for each session, you are advised to focus on only one or two of the elements that are listed below.

- Why does Mrs Collins choose Bill to take the key to the office? Do children like being chosen for errands? Why?
- Ask the children what they would have done in choosing which toilet to go into if they had been in Bill's position. Look at the illustration of Bill going into the toilet. Choosing which toilet to go into is a dilemma. Why is Bill keen to go to the toilet before he takes the key back? (It's quiet, he has time to think, there is no one about, he actually needs to use the toilet.) Do the children find this scene funny? Encourage them to imagine how Bill would feel if some girls came in while he was in there.
- How does the author add to the tension? (Everything that Bill is given has a particular problem that comes with it: the ink is in breakable glass bottles, the forms are in a special order, the balls will roll and bounce.)
- Ask the children to find examples in the text that show how adults behave towards Bill. (They don't expect him to refuse to take any of the things to the office, even those who can see he already has a lot of awkward things to carry.)
- How does Bill manage all the tasks he's been given?
- Is there any way in which Bill might have made the job of carrying everything easier? Why didn't he ask for help?
- Did the children feel sorry for Bill in this chapter? Ask them to explain why.

Ask the children, whenever appropriate, to revisit the text to exemplify/support their answers.

Encourage the children to read aloud to the group when referring back to the text – praise clear, confident and expressive reading.

Before the next session

Ask the children to read the first half of Chapter 5, up to 'through a dangerous war zone'. Ask them to take note of the titles of the comics mentioned in this section, and how they might link to boys or girls.

ASSESSMENT OPPORTUNITIES

The following bank of question prompts provides a quick and easy means of monitoring the children's comprehension skills and understanding of the text. The children's answers to a question must be supported by evidence from the text.

Understanding

- Where did Bill choose to go first after he left the classroom?
- What was Bill referring to when he asked 'How can you? How *can* you?'
- What things did Bill think pockets were useful for?
- What happened to the dress as Bill was searching to see if it had any pockets?
- List the things Bill was given to take to the office.
- What made Bill drop everything when he reached the office?

Inferences

- What do you think might have happened if the headteacher had seen Bill coming out of the girls' toilets?
- How do you think Bill feels when the headteacher's hand touches his head? Explain why you say this.
- How do you think Bill feels when each new thing is added to the pile he has to carry?
- How do you think Bill feels when he drops everything? Who does he blame?

Main ideas

- Describe the attitude of the adults towards Bill in Chapter 4.

Language, structure and presentation

- Which of these words best describes the meaning of the word 'dawdling': 'unhurried' or 'fast'?
- What do you think it means when the author says that Bill will 'risk hoots and catcalls' if he is caught in the boys' toilets wearing a dress?
- Bill's frock is described as having 'imitation' lace on it. Think of another word for 'imitation'.
- What are 'pleats, frills, bows, scallops, fancy loops' to do with in this story?

Themes and conventions

- Explain what you think the author's message is in this chapter.

▼ SESSION 4: THE BIG FIGHT

SESSION AIMS

Consider gender differences between boys and girls and see how tension and atmosphere are created.

BEFORE THE SESSION

The children should have read Chapter 5, up to 'dangerous war zone', and have noted comic titles, linking them either to boys or to girls.

READ

- Begin the session by inviting the children to share their lists of comics, saying why they think each is designed for either boys or girls. Many of the comics mentioned are now out of publication. Does their title make it easy or hard to decide the audience they are aimed at? What does this tell us about when the book was written or set?

- Ask: *Did you notice which comics Melissa and Flora were reading?* (*The Beano* and *The Dandy*.) *Are these usually thought of as boys' or girls' comics? Why do you think the author chose to draw attention to the girls reading them?*

- Why did they think that Bill became absorbed in reading *Bunty*, which was a girls' comic? Was he surprised by the stories?

- Are the children readers of comics? Invite them to describe the contents of their favourite comics. (It is often thought that girls' comics have stories while boys' focus on facts, but this is not necessarily the case – often girls' comics or magazines have a high factual content while boys' frequently include many stories, often of a fantasy or adventure nature.)

- Ask the children to look at the opening three paragraphs of the chapter. Draw attention to how the teacher's mood reflects the description of the weather, setting the atmosphere for what follows.

- Ask the children to read to the end of Chapter 5 independently.

During reading

- Ask them to keep in mind the question: *What devices does the author use to build tension and anticipation?*

- If your school uses reading journals then the children should be encouraged to make notes as they read and consider each question.

- Move around the group and 'tune in' to hear individuals read aloud. Encourage and praise good expression.

REVISIT AND RESPOND

Use the following discussion points to help the children think about what they have read in more depth.

Note: Since there are only 20 minutes for each session, you are advised to focus on only one or two of the elements that are listed below.

- Why does Mrs Collins slip into 'one of her dark wet-break moods'? Discuss with the children whether anyone enjoys wet breaks. Why might they be awful for some teachers? Why might they be awful for some children?

- At what point of the story do you realise that there's going to be a fight? Discuss the use of italics, exclamation marks and capital letters. Can children see that this helps to build up the atmosphere and tension? Take turns to read some of these sections aloud using expressive voices. How do the children think they should read 'How *dare* you?' and 'How DARE you?'? Discuss how the different features of presentation affect how you read the story.

- Who do you blame for the fight? Who starts it? Do both characters deserve to be punished?

- What do you think the reactions of the onlookers would be, when they see a boy and a girl fighting?

- Was the fight justified? Could it have been avoided?

- Focus on the final sentences, where the other children see Rohan and Bill as having different feelings after their fight. What are the differences between being '*angry*' and being '*upset*', and how do they link to gender?

Ask the children, whenever appropriate, to revisit the text to exemplify/support their answers.

Encourage the children to read aloud to the group when referring back to the text – praise clear, confident and expressive reading.

Before the next session
Ask the children to read Chapter 6, about the race, up to 'My ankle's gone all wobbly. I can't run at all'. Ask them to predict what will happen in the rest of the race, based on their knowledge of Bill.

ASSESSMENT OPPORTUNITIES
The following bank of question prompts provides a quick and easy means of monitoring the children's comprehension skills and understanding of the text. The children's answers to a question must be supported by evidence from the text.

Understanding
- Why were the children all reading comics in the classroom?
- Why did Bill think the dress was 'a silly curse'?
- What did the other children do when Bill and Rohan began to fight?
- What was Mrs Collins' reaction to Bill and Rohan fighting?
- Who is angry at the end? Who is upset?
- Do you think Mrs Collins' treatment of Rohan is fair? Why do you say that?

Inferences
- Do you think Mrs Collins has good reason to be angry with the class when they are choosing from the comic box? Explain why you say that.
- Is Bill first or last to receive a comic from Mrs Collins? How do you know that?
- Why do you think Bill does not want to read Bunty when it is given to him?

Predicting
- What do you think might happen next time there is a wet playtime?
- What do you think Bill might feel about the different comics in the future? Why?

Main ideas
- Why do you think Anne Fine chose to include a chapter that had boys' and girls' comics as the focus? What point was she making?
- What point do you think the author is making when she describes how the other children think Rohan is 'angry' but Bill is 'upset' after the fight?

Language, structure and presentation
- What does the author mean by 'wet-break'?
- How do you know that Mrs Collins is angry with the class when they are choosing comics?
- The comics are 'shabby and dog-eared'. Explain why you think the author uses the description 'dog-eared' here.
- Give an example of the author's use of descriptive language that really helped you to visualise what was happening. Explain how this language helped you.

Themes and conventions
- Suggest what the differences might be between comics aimed at girls and those designed for boys.

▼ SESSION 5: LETTING PAUL WIN

SESSION AIMS

Predict outcomes and evaluate character motivations.

BEFORE THE SESSION

The children should have read part of Chapter 6, up to 'I can't run at all'. They should be prepared to discuss their predictions about what will happen in the rest of the chapter.

READ

- Begin by asking the children for their predictions about what will happen in the rest of the race, giving reasons for their suggestions.

- Ask: *Why do you think Mrs Collins organised the races in the way that she did?* (To try and make them fairer.) Ask them to find some of the ways in which the races were categorised by Mrs Collins (light-haired against dark-haired, straight-haired against curly-haired, those who put out rubbish in wheely-bins and those who use plastic bags).

- What is the children's opinion of the teacher sending Paul off to run in a heat of his own? Is this a good idea? Is it fair? Why? (Note: if you have disabled children in your group, treat this sensitively.)

  - Could Mrs Collins have done anything else to make Paul feel included?

  - Why do the girls make their plan? Bill is not really listening – why not?

  - What do you think of the girls' plan? Why do you think that?

- Skim the opening pages, looking for the author's verb choices, such as 'sailed', 'blazed', 'steamed', 'reflected', 'astonished', 'ignored', 'offering', 'slid', 'spilled', 'overlooked' and 'imprisoned'. Ask the children why they think Anne Fine chose these particular verbs. What others might she have used? Why are these effective? (They have been chosen deliberately over simpler verbs, adding interest and variety.)

- Ask the children to read on to the end of Chapter 6 independently.

During reading

- Ask them to consider the motives of the girls and Bill during the race.

- If your school uses reading journals then the children should be encouraged to make notes as they read and consider each question.

- Move around the group and 'tune in' to hear individuals read aloud. Encourage and praise good expression.

REVISIT AND RESPOND

Use the following discussion points to help the children think about what they have read in more depth.

Note: Since there are only 20 minutes for each session, you are advised to focus on only one or two of the elements that are listed below.

- Bill is told what the plan is and he does agree to it, but when he's racing he cannot let Paul win. Encourage the children to think about all the reasons for this. Why is it better in the end that Bill does win the race?

- What were the girls' reasons for fixing the race? Do the children think this was a good idea? Do they think Paul would realise what they had done? If he did, how would that make him feel towards them?

- What is the children's opinion of how Bill behaves during the race?

- What do they think the girls' opinion of Bill would be after the race?

- Ask the children to explain what they liked about the way the race was described, choosing sections they thought were particularly effective and explaining their choice.

- Ask the children if Anne Fine suggests that it is wrong to be competitive, giving their reasons for their thoughts.

- Do they think that Bill behaves more like a boy in deciding to win the race?

Ask the children, whenever appropriate, to revisit the text to exemplify/support their answers.

Encourage the children to read aloud to the group when referring back to the text – praise clear, confident and expressive reading.

Before the next session
Ask the children to skim-read the first six chapters of the book before the final session, making notes about how Bill's dilemma affected him during the day. Ask them to consider how Bill's attitude towards both girls and boys might change because of his experiences. Invite them to predict how the story will end – will Bill remain as a girl?

ASSESSMENT OPPORTUNITIES
The following bank of question prompts provides a quick and easy means of monitoring the children's comprehension skills and understanding of the text. The children's answers to a question must be supported by evidence from the text.

Understanding
- Why did Mrs Collins decide to take the class outside to have some races?
- How did Bill's frock make racing difficult for him?
- Explain the girls' plan for the race.
- Who came first in the race and who came second?
- Why did Kirsty think it might have been for the best that Paul didn't win the race in the end?
- After the races Kirsty thinks Bill seems *different*. Why is this? What does it mean?

Inferences
- How do we know that the children were pleased to go out and have the races?
- How do you think Paul would feel when he is sent off to race on his own? Why do you think this?
- How did Paul feel when he won his heat? How do you know?

Main ideas
- This chapter gives the opportunity to consider the motives of Mrs Collins in deciding to have the races and in sending Paul off to race on his own, the

motives of the girls in planning to let Paul win and of Bill in deciding to race properly so that Paul wouldn't win. Can the children offer some suggestions of what these motives might have been?

Language, structure and presentation
- What does Kirsty mean when she accuses Bill of not listening because he is 'away with the fairies'?
- 'He was already halfway round the circuit'. Explain what a 'circuit' is.
- 'A smile of triumph spread across his face. He'd won.' Suggest another word for 'triumph'.

Themes and conventions
- What does the girls' plan suggest about how girls react to others? Would boys be likely to do the same thing? Is it fair that the author has chosen a group of girls to plan to help Paul win the race? Is she herself using stereotypical behaviour and attitudes here? How do boy readers feel about this?

SESSION 6: HAPPY ENDING

SESSION AIMS

Evaluate the story and reach conclusions about gender differences.

BEFORE THE SESSION

The children should have skim-read the first six chapters.

READ

- Before they begin reading the final chapter, ask the children for their predictions of how the story will end. Do they think Bill will remain as a girl? Will he *want* to stay as a girl?

- Invite the children to recall as many incidents as they can from the story relating to how wearing the dress affected Bill during the day. How would they sum up Bill's day so far? Was there any part of it that he enjoyed? For example: when he arrived late at the school gates, he wasn't told off like the boys were; he found that he did quite enjoy reading a girls' comic; and he might initially have enjoyed being chosen to leave the lesson to take things to the school office.

- Ask the children to read Chapter 7 independently.

During reading

- Look together at the chapter title: 'Happy ending'. Ask: *What does this suggest the story ending might be?*

- As they read the final chapter, ask the children to consider how Bill's experiences over the whole day might affect him in the future.

- If your school uses reading journals then the children should be encouraged to make notes as they read and consider each question.

- Move around the group and 'tune in' to hear individuals read aloud. Encourage and praise good expression.

REVISIT AND RESPOND

Use the following discussion points to help the children think about what they have read in more depth.

Note: Since there are only 20 minutes for each session, you are advised to focus on only one or two of the elements that are listed below.

- Did the children predict the ending correctly? Are they satisfied that Bill once again became a boy?

- Refer to the paragraph beginning 'He had his doubts, though'. Draw attention to the words 'dispirited', 'trailed' and 'dragging', used to describe Bill, and 'jumping' and 'excitedly', used to describe Paul, and compare them. Talk about how careful word choice suggests rather than tells us how a character is feeling, making the writing stronger and more interesting.

- How is Bill feeling on his way home? Think about how Bill feels in the morning when he passes Mean Malcolm. Can the children explain why Bill reacts as he does to Malcolm's whistle on the way home? Do the children approve of the way that Bill reacts? Why? Which is the better way to react to Malcolm – as Bill does on the way to school or as he does on his way home? Can the children come up with a really good solution for dealing with Malcolm? Would ignoring Malcolm work?

- When he fights Mean Malcolm, this is Bill's second fight of the day. Ask: *Do you think Bill is often involved in fights? What do the two fights tell us about how he is feeling on this particular day?*

- Ask the children to read the short section near the end of the book, starting with 'Bill needed no prompting' up to 'such relief'. Ask: *How has the author slowed down the action here to show us how Bill is feeling?'*

- Discuss the story as a whole. What is Anne Fine trying to do? Does she succeed? Can the children summarise how Bill might have changed as a result of his extraordinary day?

- Do the children think that Bill might treat girls – and boys – any differently after his experiences? Might he try to persuade others to behave differently?

- Do they think Bill would ever tell anyone about what happened to him? Why, or why not?
- Ask the children why they think it is considered acceptable for girls to wear trousers but not for boys to wear skirts or dresses.

Ask the children, whenever appropriate, to revisit the text to exemplify/support their answers.

Encourage the children to read aloud to the group when referring back to the text – praise clear, confident and expressive reading.

ASSESSMENT OPPORTUNITIES

The following bank of question prompts provides a quick and easy means of monitoring the children's comprehension skills and understanding of the text. The children's answers to a question must be supported by evidence from the text.

Understanding

- Has your opinion of Mrs Collins as a teacher altered by the end of the story? Explain why you say that.
- How could the state of Bill's dress be said to tell the story of his day?
- When he meets Mean Malcolm on the way home, Bill yells that he is 'a *person*!'. Why has the author chosen to use the word 'person' instead of 'boy' here?

Inferences

- How do we know that Bill was eager to return back to being a boy?
- Why do you think Bill reacts in the way that he does to Mean Malcolm's whistle the second time?

Predicting

- Imagine Bill's next day at school, describing how he might behave towards both girls and boys.
- Would Mean Malcolm behave in the same way towards Bill the next time they meet? Give your reasons.
- How might Bill's experiences help to make him a more understanding person in the future?
- How might Bill's experiences help him to deal better with difficulties in the future?

Main ideas

- Do you agree with the author's view about gender in this story? Give reasons why you say this.
- Do you think a person can be judged by the clothes they wear? Give reasons for your opinion.

Language, structure and presentation

- Why might Anne Fine have decided to limit Bill's experiences to just one day? How does this impact on the story?
- Why do you think Mean Malcolm 'looked astonished to find this pink apparition glaring at him with such menace'?
- Look at the words printed in italics in this chapter and explain why the author chose to italicise them.
- Throughout the story, none of the other characters calls Bill by a name. Why do you think the author chose to do this?

Themes and conventions

- Do you think boys and girls should be treated differently? Explain why you say that.

SESSION 1: DARK IS EXCITING

SESSION AIMS

Consider how the character of Plop is created by the author and introduces the main theme.

BEFORE THE SESSION

The children should have read Chapter 1 'Dark is exciting' independently prior to the session, and looked at images of barn owls and barn owl chicks.

READ

- Ask for volunteers to read the first few pages of the book (up to 'Plop waited.')
- Ask:
  - Who is Plop?
  - Who are the other main characters so far?
  - Where does Plop live?
  - *What is the problem that Plop has?*
- Agree the key dilemma of the story is the fact that Plop – who is a night bird – is afraid of the dark. Introduce the word *nocturnal* to the children. Discuss how being a day bird would change Plop's life. (He would have to find different things to eat, he wouldn't see his family, he wouldn't be able to find a mate, and so on.)
- Ask: *What happens in this first chapter to start the story?* (Plop's mother decides that he needs to learn about the dark and sends him out of the nest to talk to people.) Discuss with the children:
  - Who is the first person that Plop meets?
  - What does he say?
  - Why does the boy think that the dark is exciting?
- Encourage the children to describe what they think will happen next to Plop, justifying their answers. Ask them to make longer-term predictions about Plop: do they think that he will learn to love the dark, or will his parents let him become a day bird?

REVISIT AND RESPOND

Use the following discussion points to help the children think about what they have read in more depth.

Note: Since there are only 20 minutes for each session, you are advised to focus on only one or two of the elements that are listed below.

- Look together at the image of Plop on the front cover. Remind the children of the images of baby barn owls that they looked at before the session. Ask volunteers to describe Plop, encouraging the children to build on each other's thoughts. Ask: *How do we relate to Plop? What does the author do to make him so appealing?* Tell the children to work with a partner to find passages where Jill Tomlinson describes how Plop looks, how he moves and what he says. Share the children's ideas and agree that the author makes Plop extremely sweet; she makes him quite adorable and vulnerable through:
  - description: 'fat and fluffy', 'beautiful heart-shaped ruff', 'enormous, round eyes', 'knackety knees';
  - his behaviour: afraid of the dark, looks at his toes, flies very badly;
  - how he talks: his incorrect grammar and vocabulary use makes him seem very young and cute – for example, 'What I are is afraid of the dark' and 'I might spill myself'.
- Ask the children to share their ideas on what sort of knees 'knackety' knees might be, and what Plop means when he says he might 'spill' himself.
- Provide the children with a small whiteboard between pairs and ask each pair to find the different descriptions of fireworks in the chapter, noting down the page numbers. Share the different descriptions the children have found. Allow time for the children to discuss their own experience of watching fireworks, which are their favourites and whether they find them exciting or frightening. Encourage them to use different adjectives to describe the fireworks they have seen and the sounds they made. Ask: *Do you think that Plop's*

mother is right? Will Plop be less scared of the dark if he understands it? Does watching the fireworks make Plop less scared of the night? (No, it teaches him to love fireworks and see that dark is useful but it doesn't really help him.)

- Ask the children: *What are you frightened of?* Allow time for the children to talk about the things that they are frightened of, sharing a few of your own phobias (real or imaginary). Encourage the children to listen sensitively to each other. Help them to understand that while someone else's phobias might seem rather silly or childish, to that person they will be very real and reasonable and that we should always be very kind and understanding about someone else's fears. At the same time, we can try different techniques to confront our own fears, such as learning more about them, and that will help us to control – or even overcome – them.

- Explain that overcoming a fear through learning about it is the main theme of the story. Remind the children that a theme is a main idea that is explored in a story. Ask a volunteer to re-read the conversation between Plop and his mother in the first few pages of the book (from 'You *can't* be afraid of the dark…' to '…before you make up your mind about it'.) Ask:

  - What is the difference between knowing and feeling?
  - Do you think Plop's mother is right?
  - What colour is the night sky?

Ask the children, whenever appropriate, to revisit the text to exemplify/support their answers.

Encourage the children to read aloud to the group when referring back to the text – praise clear, confident and expressive reading.

Before the next session
Ask the children to read Chapter 2 'Dark is kind'.

ASSESSMENT OPPORTUNITIES
The following bank of question prompts provides a quick and easy means of monitoring the children's comprehension skills and understanding of the text. The children's answers to a question must be supported by evidence from the text.

Understanding
- What sort of owl is Plop?
- What does he look like?
- Why does he go and talk to the boy?
- Why does it need to be dark for fireworks?

Inferences
- What does Plop's mother think of his fears?
- What does Plop think about the fireworks?
- Why does the boy think that Plop is a Catherine-wheel?

Predicting
- Will watching the fireworks help Plop to like the dark?
- Chapter 2 is called 'Dark is kind'. How do you think dark can be kind?

Main ideas
- What are the three main events in this chapter?

Language, structure and presentation
- What do you think the word 'knackety' means?

Themes and conventions
- What is Plop frightened of?
- Do you think it helps to find out about something you are frightened of?

▼ SESSION 2: DARK IS KIND

SESSION AIMS

Consider Plop and his relationship with his family, and the old lady and her memories.

BEFORE THE SESSION

The children should have read Chapter 2 'Dark is kind' independently prior to the session.

READ

- Ask the children to recap on the main events of the story so far and to summarise what happens in this second chapter. (His parents take turns to hunt and feed him, he sleeps for a while but wakes up early and his mother tells him to go and find someone to ask about night. He talks to a very old lady about her memories.)
- Check their understanding by asking:
  - What does Plop eat?
  - Where does his food come from?
  - Who does Plop talk to while his parents sleep?
  - What does the old lady say?
  - Why does she think that dark is kind?

REVISIT AND RESPOND

Use the following discussion points to help the children think about what they have read in more depth.

Note: Since there are only 20 minutes for each session, you are advised to focus on only one or two of the elements that are listed below.

- Ask the children to find a partner and think of some words and phrases to describe Plop (inquisitive, brave about talking to people, enthusiastic, fun, hungry, talkative). Ask them to share their thoughts and create a group list on a whiteboard. Then ask the children to turn back to their pairs and now think of words and phrases to describe Mrs Barn

Owl (kind, patient, frustrated, reassuring, good at explaining things). Again, share these as a group. Thirdly, ask: *What do we know about Mr Barn Owl? How does he fly?* (He 'floated' like a 'great white moth'.) Ask: *What does this tell us?* (That he is white, that he doesn't flap his wings and it suggests that he is very quiet.) *Why does he need to be quiet?*

- Re-read the conversation between the old lady and Plop, asking two volunteers to take on each role. Ensure the children have understood how the old lady feels (that she is sad about looking old, about her house being old and that she is lonely), and why she feels better in the dark (she can't see that she is old and the house is old, and she can remember happy times). Discuss whether the children think the old lady's thoughts on the dark will be helpful to Plop. (Not really as he has nothing to remember or hide and has very good eyesight.) Ask them to locate what Plop says to his mother about his conversation with the old lady. Which part does his father particularly like the sound of? Why? Explain the old lady's comment about carrots – that some people say that carrots help us to see in the dark.

- Manners are very important to the old lady. Ask the children to search for the four different ways that the old lady picks Plop up on his manners. Ask: *What does he do at the end that makes her say that he has lovely manners?* Ask: *Do you think children should be seen and not heard?*

- As a group, ask the children to compare Plop with the old lady. Draw a line down the middle of a small whiteboard and label each side. Ask: *What's the old lady like?* Tell the children to find evidence in the text – encouraging the children to use inference to improve their description (for example, tired, thoughtful, sad, lonely, full of memories, has bad eyesight, likes to remember when her children were little, likes children to be well behaved). Ask: *How is Plop different from the old lady?* (He can't sleep, is nervous, happy, has a family, no memories, great eyesight, does not have great manners.)

- Talk to the children about the happy memories they have: birthday parties, being in Reception class, Christmas plays, family outings and so on. Talk about how these memories could cheer them up when they are sad or frightened.

- Talk about what Plop has learned about the dark. Has he learned anything that could help him? Remind the children how different he is from the old lady.

Ask the children, whenever appropriate, to revisit the text to exemplify/support their answers.

Encourage the children to read aloud to the group when referring back to the text – praise clear, confident and expressive reading.

Before the next session
Ask the children to read Chapter 3 'Dark is fun'.

ASSESSMENT OPPORTUNITIES

The following bank of question prompts provides a quick and easy means of monitoring the children's comprehension skills and understanding of the text. The children's answers to a question must be supported by evidence from the text.

Understanding
- What do Plop's parents spend the night doing?
- What does the old lady think about in the dark?
- Why does the old lady think that Plop is a thunderbolt?

Inferences
- Why does Plop's mother suggest that he go and find someone to talk to?
- What does the old lady feel sad about?

Predicting
- Will Plop find the old lady's thoughts about the dark useful?

Main ideas
- Summarise the two main events of the chapter.
- Explain how Plop's parents feed him.

Language, structure and presentation
- What is the 'little word' that the old lady thinks 'works wonders'?
- How does the author describe Plop's father flying in the night?

SESSION 3: DARK IS FUN

SESSION AIMS

Understand how conversation is used to move on the plot, and infer feelings and character.

BEFORE THE SESSION

The children should have read Chapter 3 'Dark is fun' independently prior to the session.

READ

- Ask the children to help you remember what happens in this chapter. Agree that Plop meets a Boy Scout and joins in with the fun around the camp-fire. Challenge the children to remember what happens before he meets the Boy Scout (his father invites him to go hunting, he refuses and spends the time waiting for his parents, practising remembering). Challenge the children to find the following details in the text:
  - How is Plop's father described as he flies off to hunt?
  - What does Plop remember as he sits waiting for his parents?
  - What does the Boy Scout think Plop is when he lands?
  - Which Boy Scout is always the first to be caught?
  - What two new things does Plop eat in this chapter?

REVISIT AND RESPOND

Use the following discussion points to help the children think about what they have read in more depth.

Note: Since there are only 20 minutes for each session, you are advised to focus on only one or two of the elements that are listed below.

- Ask: *What did Plop learn about in this chapter?* (Games humans can play in the dark, camp-fires that humans can have, camp food that humans eat.) Ask: *Did he learn about the dark? Did the Boy Scout help Plop to understand the dark?* Invite the

children to discuss their thoughts with a partner before sharing their ideas with the group. Help the children to articulate different sides to the argument: he's learning to have fun in the dark, which will make him less scared in future; he's only learning about the human experience of the dark; he's learning about lights in the dark, not the dark itself; he's staying up late in the dark. Insist that the children listen to each other's point of view, praising any child that builds on something that someone else says.

- Point out to the children that much of the story is told through speech. Give each of the children a different page from the chapter (apart from the one page with no speech) and ask them to find words that are spoken out loud on their page. Tell each child to read out the line of speech – only reading the words that are spoken out loud. Use a whiteboard and one of the lines read out to recap on the rules of writing speech, clarifying any confusion with double and single quotes and the rules that you would like them to use in their own writing. As a group, go through the chapter and note all the information that we find out through speech: what Mrs Barn Owl wants Plop to do, what Plop looks like when he lands, what the Boy Scout tells us about games and camp-fires, what Plop eats at night and so on.

- Ask: *Who has had a camp-fire on holiday or at home?* Encourage the children to share any experiences they have, including through the Cubs or Brownies. Talk about any food that the children have cooked on a camp-fire, or a barbeque. Ask those children who are Beavers or Rainbows, Cubs or Brownies, or who have siblings in the Scouts or Guides, to talk about the uniform they wear and games they play and any camps that they have been on.

- Ask: *What does the Boy Scout feel as he sits listening to his friends playing in the woods? What phrase tells us that he is a bit jealous or fed up?* ('Oh, it *would* be my turn to guard the fire.') Ask: *Why is the word 'would' in italics?* Ask volunteers to demonstrate reading this line putting the emphasis on the word 'would'. Can they try out different ways of saying this line: moany, wistful, cross, putting a brave face on, and so on. Challenge the children to find other emotions in the chapter, encouraging them to infer where needed: Plop's brave feelings as he waits in the dark, Plop's happiness round the camp-fire, the Boy Scouts playing the games, Mrs Barn Owl's feelings when Plop tells her about the fun he's had but that he still hates the dark.

Ask the children, whenever appropriate, to revisit the text to exemplify/support their answers.

Encourage the children to read aloud to the group when referring back to the text – praise clear, confident and expressive reading.

Before the next session
Ask the children to read Chapter 4 'Dark is necessary'.

ASSESSMENT OPPORTUNITIES
The following bank of question prompts provides a quick and easy means of monitoring the children's comprehension skills and understanding of the text. The children's answers to a question must be supported by evidence from the text.

Understanding
- What did Plop's mother look like as she flew off to hunt?
- Describe one of the games that the Boy Scouts play.
- Why does Plop need to wait for the potato to cool down?
- Why is the Boy Scout waiting by the fire on his own?

Inferences
- How did Plop feel when the darkness came towards him and wrapped itself around him?
- How do we know that Plop rolls when he lands?
- How does the Boy Scout feel about the fire?
- Why is Plop so interested in food?

Predicting
- Will Plop's fun at the camp-fire stop him being scared of the dark?

Main ideas
- Why did the Boy Scout think that dark is FUN?

Language, structure and presentation
- The Boy Scout says that playing games in the dark is 'super'. Where does Plop use this word?

Themes and conventions
- In what different ways is Plop brave?

SESSION 4: DARK IS NECESSARY

SESSION AIMS

Consider the effects of asking and answering questions and the repetitive structure of the chapters.

BEFORE THE SESSION

The children should have read Chapter 4 'Dark is necessary' independently prior to the session.

READ

- Ask the children to explain the main events of this chapter. Help the children to make the link between the squirrel at the opening of this chapter and the squirrels that live in the same tree as Plop. (Help the children to find the point in the first chapter when Plop says he lives in the 'top flat'.) Ask: *Why might the squirrel be frightened of Plop?*

- Invite a child to read out loud the passage where Plop lands by the little girl.

During reading

- Ask: *How do we know that Plop is getting better at landing?*

- Invite the children to visualise the scene as the little girl finds her presents on Christmas morning. Ask: *What does she do first?*

- Point out that the little girl and Plop both think that a real mouse is a better gift than a sugar mouse. Ask: *Why does the little girl want a mouse? Why does Plop?*

- If your school uses reading journals then the children should be encouraged to make notes as they read and consider each question.

- Move around the group and 'tune in' to hear individuals read aloud. Encourage and praise good expression.

REVISIT AND RESPOND

Use the following discussion points to help the children think about what they have read in more depth.

Note: Since there are only 20 minutes for each session, you are advised to focus on only one or two of the elements that are listed below.

- Ask: *What questions does Plop ask in this chapter? How does this help him learn about the dark and the little girl's feelings about the dark?* Challenge the children to ask their own questions about barn owls, noting them down on a small whiteboard. Allow them to start with questions they know the answer to, in order to practise writing questions. Then challenge them to generate questions that they genuinely want to know the answer to. Encourage them to think about where barn owls live, when they lay their eggs, when their eggs hatch, how parent barn owls look after their young, where you can see a barn owl. Finally, ask them to move on to asking questions about Plop, encouraging them to think about what they know about Plop already and then to think deeper about Plop, his fears and his bravery.

- Tell the children to work with a partner to find out as much about barn owls as they can, using the information in the book. If you have carried out the activity above, then use the questions generated to enthuse their search. If not, tell the children to think about food, habitat, when they leave the nest, how they move, how they sleep, how they fly, what noise they make and so on. Ask: *Can you work out from the book what time of year barn owl chicks are born?* (Help them to see that the book is set in Autumn and that Plop is eight weeks old.)

- Talk about the children's experience of waiting for Father Christmas, or the Tooth Fairy, the night before their birthday or other festivals where they get presents. Talk about the excitement of waiting for it to get dark and then lying in bed at night. Contrast these feelings with not wanting the next day to come – perhaps there is a spelling test or a trip to the dentist – and wanting it to stay dark. Talk about festivals where dark is necessary, such as Bonfire Night, Diwali or Hanukkah.

- Ask the children to help you summarise the events of this chapter: Plop's parents go hunting; Plop sleeps for a while; Plop wakes, screeches and wakes his mother, who tells him to find someone to talk to; Plop talks to the little girl; he comes back and tells his mother. Write this on the whiteboard. Ask the children to work with a partner to summarise the events of one of the previous two chapters (organise the group so that both chapters are covered). Share the summaries, noting them down next to the summary for this chapter. Help the children to see how similar the structures of these chapters are. Ask: *Do you know any other stories where similar things happen a number of times?* (For example, some fairytales, such as the Golden Goose or the Little Red Hen, or a television series.) Compare this structure with the structure of other books the children have studied, particularly any that follow the traditional beginning–build-up–problem–resolution–ending, and discuss how you have looked at these stories as having a mountain structure.

Ask the children, whenever appropriate, to revisit the text to exemplify/support their answers.

Encourage the children to read aloud to the group when referring back to the text – praise clear, confident and expressive reading.

Before the next session
Ask the children to read Chapters 5 and 6, 'Dark Is fascinating' and 'Dark is wonderful'.

ASSESSMENT OPPORTUNITIES

The following bank of question prompts provides a quick and easy means of monitoring the children's comprehension skills and understanding of the text. The children's answers to a question must be supported by evidence from the text.

Understanding
- What sort of noise does a tawny owl make?
- What sort of noise does a barn owl make?
- Why was the squirrel surprised to see Plop?

Inferences
- Do you think that the little girl is afraid of the dark?
- What time of year is the story set in?

- How do Mr and Mrs Barn Owl feel about hunting for all Plop's food?

Predicting
- What do you think Father Christmas will put in Plop's stocking?
- Do you think waiting for Father Christmas will help Plop to stop being afraid of the dark?

Main ideas
- Why does the little girl say that 'DARK IS NECESSARY'?

Language, structure and presentation
- Find three places in the story so far where the way Plop talks indicates that he's very young.

▼ SESSION 5: DARK IS FASCINATING AND WONDERFUL

SESSION AIMS

Consider the mini theme of hunting in these two chapters.

BEFORE THE SESSION

The children should have read Chapters 5 'Dark is fascinating' and 6 'Dark is wonderful'; they also need to have looked at images of badgers, hedgehogs and bats, and images of the constellation Orion.

READ

- Ask the children to remember what happens in Chapter 5 'Dark is fascinating'. Ask:
  - Who thinks that dark is fascinating?
  - What is the girl really fascinated in?
  - What animals does she talk about?
  - What sort of animals are these?

- Remind the children of the word 'nocturnal' and tell them to imagine the night-time setting of *The Owl Who Was Afraid of the Dark*, with different animals (including those animals such as shrews, mice and grasshoppers that Plop's father catches) creeping, scuttling or flying around at night. Ask: *How might this make Plop feel?* Perhaps it would make him feel that night was a busy place – and therefore not very frightening.

- Ask the children to now remember the events of Chapter 6 'Dark is wonderful'. Allow time for the children to share any experiences they have of seeing the stars clearly (tricky if you live in the city).

- Ask: *Have the two people Plop met in the last two chapters helped Plop to understand the dark more than the people he met in the first chapters?* (Possibly, yes, as they have helped him to understand his own world, rather than the world of humans.)

- Encourage the children to compare the structure of these two chapters with the previous chapters, asking them to find elements that are the same in

each – for example, talks to his parents, lands in a funny way, talks to a human, screeches, tells his mother, eats something.

REVISIT AND RESPOND

Use the following discussion points to help the children think about what they have read in more depth.

Note: Since there are only 20 minutes for each session, you are advised to focus on only one or two of the elements that are listed below.

- Tell the children to search these two chapters to find clues that Plop is growing up (for example, begins to look like his father, starting to land better, his screech sounds 'gorgeous', sleeps during the day). Ask: *What does this mean for Plop? Might this mean that he is ready to like the dark and become a proper barn owl?*

- Ask: *Who can remember any descriptions of how Plop flies? Who can remember how Mr Barn Owl flies?* As a group, find all the descriptions of flight in the book – about Plop and his parents. Challenge them to find references to the landing branch. What do they think that is? Ask: *Which form of flight is best for hunting? Why? What will Plop need to do before he can become a great hunter?*

- Ask the children if they can remember the word we used to describe animals that are active at night. Draw up a list of all the nocturnal animals that the children can remember (including those not in the book, such as foxes). Ask: *Why do you think some animals hunt at night? Why do other animals come out at night?* Explain that there are fewer animals out at night and it is harder to see them, so some animals are safer coming out at night and some predators have less competition for food or only eat nocturnal animals.

- Discuss how people used to use the stars (particularly the Pole Star) to navigate at night and to know the passing of the seasons. Ask: *Do you think that the barn owls use this system?* (No, they are very confused by it.) If your area is rural enough, then challenge the children to spot Orion, if it is the right time of year. Ask: *Why is Orion a good constellation for Plop to learn?* (Because he is a hunter that is seen at night.) If you are in a town, talk about the moon and ask the children to see what shape the moon is at the moment. Ask if anyone's ever seen a shooting star, sharing any anecdotes. Explain that shooting stars – or meteors – are rocks burning up in the Earth's atmosphere.

Ask the children, whenever appropriate, to revisit the text to exemplify/support their answers.

Encourage the children to read aloud to the group when referring back to the text – praise clear, confident and expressive reading.

Before the next session
Ask the children to read Chapter 7 'Dark is beautiful'.

ASSESSMENT OPPORTUNITIES

The following bank of question prompts provides a quick and easy means of monitoring the children's comprehension skills and understanding of the text. The children's answers to a question must be supported by evidence from the text.

Understanding
- What is Orion?
- Why does the hedgehog not worry about being quiet?
- How does the lady artist distinguish between the animals at the front of her notebook and the animals at the back?
- What is another name for a meteor?

Inferences
- Why is Plop beginning to sleep through the day?
- Why does the lady like night animals so much?

Predicting
- Will knowing about nocturnal animals help Plop to love the dark?
- Will knowing about stars help Plop to love the dark?

Main ideas
- Why does the man with the telescope think that dark is wonderful?

Language, structure and presentation
- Name two things that happen the same in every chapter you have read so far.

Themes and conventions
- How does the hedgehog stop itself from being hunted?
- How is Plop like Orion?

▼ SESSION 6: DARK IS BEAUTIFUL

Consider the ending of the story, matching it against original predictions and themes, and noting changes across the book.

BEFORE THE SESSION

The children should have read Chapter 7 'Dark is beautiful' independently before the session.

READ

- Ask: *How is this chapter different from the rest? How does Plop feel when he first wakes up? What does he think about his parents sleeping?* Tell the children to find the description of Plop landing. Ask: *How does Plop land this time? How does this compare to his previous landings? How does this description compare with some of the descriptions of Plop's father?*

- Ask: *Who does Plop meet in this chapter?* Point out that the cat is another animal who likes the night – whereas his other conversations were with humans.

- Ask two volunteers to read aloud the section of this chapter that covers Plop's time with the cat.

During reading

- While reading, ask: *What do Plop and the cat talk about? Where do they go? What is the setting like?*

- If your school uses reading journals then the children should be encouraged to make notes as they read and consider each question.

- Move around the group and 'tune in' to hear individuals read aloud. Encourage and praise good expression.

- Agree that this conversation is about the night itself rather than an activity during the night; instead of just standing under Plop's tree, Plop and the cat go exploring high up in the urban (town) landscape.

- Ask: *How does Plop overcome his fear of the dark?* (He learns that it is beautiful in itself.) Point out the phrase: 'This is my world.' He has become who he was supposed to be – a night bird. Help the children

to link the ending to the themes of fear, the night being a good thing and deciding who we are and what we like.

REVISIT AND RESPOND

Use the following discussion points to help the children think about what they have read in more depth.

Note: Since there are only 20 minutes for each session, you are advised to focus on only one or two of the elements that are listed below.

- Ask the children to discuss their original predictions for the book. Ask: *Who predicted that Plop would learn to love the dark? How did the events differ from your expectations? Has the book changed your own attitude to the dark? Can you see more beauty in it now? Will you look for more night-time colours? Would you like to play games in the dark (like the Boy Scouts did), go star gazing or look for nocturnal animals? If you were afraid of the dark, would the story stop you being afraid?*

- Ask the group to return to the beginning of the book and re-read the description of Plop and then skim-read the first conversations he has with his mother and with the boy who likes fireworks. Ask: *How does Plop change over the course of the story?* Ask each child to suggest a way in which Plop has changed (for example, his speech, his landings, his screech, his attitude to the dark, wanting to go hunting, silent flying, being prepared to go far from the nest, sleeping during the day, and so on). Go back to Chapter 3 'Dark is fun' and point out the phrase 'The darkness seemed to come towards him and wrap itself around him'. Then ask: *How does he feel about the dark now?*

- Remind the children that a theme is a main idea in a story. Agree that the main theme in this story is overcoming a fear through finding out information, but point out that 'the night' is another theme. Ask a volunteer to read the cat's description of different types of night. Invite the children to list the different kinds of night that are described. Tell the children to think of and describe further types of night, such as misty nights, windy nights, muggy nights, drizzly nights and so on. Then put a large drop of black ink onto a piece of blotting paper and watch the black separate out into different colours. Invite the children to tell you all the colours that Plop sees in the book. Ask: *What colours does Plop's mother say the night is in the first chapter?* Challenge them to find as many white things in the chapter as they can (for example, Plop, snow, frost, stars, the white moon on the lake, lightning). Ask: *What other white things are mentioned earlier in the book?* (Plop's father like a white moth or statue, the stars.) Note down and talk about the descriptive noun phrases used in this final chapter.

- Remind the children that Mrs Barn Owl tells Plop in the first chapter that he doesn't like the night because he is relying on his feelings rather than his knowledge and that he needs to find out about the night to stop being so frightened of it. Ask the children to discuss whether, at the end of the book, they think she is right. At the end, is it Plop's knowledge or feelings that have changed?

Ask the children, whenever appropriate, to revisit the text to exemplify/support their answers.

Encourage the children to read aloud to the group when referring back to the text – praise clear, confident and expressive reading.

ASSESSMENT OPPORTUNITIES

The following bank of question prompts provides a quick and easy means of monitoring the children's comprehension skills and understanding of the text. The children's answers to a question must be supported by evidence from the text.

Understanding
- What does the cat tell Plop about the night time?
- What is the cat's name?
- What happens at the very end of the book?

Inferences
- Why do Plop's parents pretend to be asleep when Plop is shouting at the darkness at the beginning of the chapter?
- How do Plop's parents feel when he says that he likes the dark?

Predicting
- Will Plop be frightened of the dark ever again?
- Will Plop visit his human friends again?

Main ideas
- What is the main idea of the last chapter?

Language, structure and presentation
- What repetitive phrase is used for all of the chapter headings?
- Find two noun phrases in this chapter.

Themes and conventions
- What is the main theme of the book?
- What is another theme of the book?

▼ SESSION 1: MEET THE TWITS

SESSION AIMS

Identify the main ideas, drawn from various paragraphs, and draw inferences about characters.

BEFORE THE SESSION

The children should have familiarised themselves with the book's cover.

READ

- Begin with a brief group discussion on what the children have established from the book cover and title, using these questions:
  - What genre of book is it?
  - What can you tell about the storyline?
  - Who are the Twits?
- Then, ask the group to read together the first four short chapters, keeping the following questions in mind:
  - According to Mr Twit, what is his best feature?
  - Is there anything likeable about Mr Twit?
  - In what way is Mrs Twit similar to her husband?
  - What is the author's opinion of the Twits?

During reading

- Compare the pictures to the descriptions of the characters.
- Identify who is telling the story (the author is also the narrator).
- If your school uses reading journals then the children should be encouraged to make notes as they read and consider each question.
- Move around the group and 'tune in' to hear individuals read aloud. Encourage and praise good expression.
- At the end, ask the children to consider this question:
  - Do Mr and Mrs Twit suit each other?

REVISIT AND RESPOND

Use the following discussion points to help the children think about what they have read in more depth.

Note: Since there are only 20 minutes for each session, you are advised to focus on only one or two of the elements that are listed below.

- Examine the way the author begins the story. Ask the children: *How would you describe the opening of the story?* (Unusual, strange, odd, silly.) *Does it get your attention? Do you think this could be an important part of the plot?*
- Ask the group to consider chapter length and see if they have noticed how short they are. Discuss why the author chose short chapters and the effect it has, especially for younger readers.
- Notice that the author addresses the reader directly. Ask the children to find examples in the text. Ask: *How does the author use this technique to connect with readers, and separate himself and readers from the characters?* (He implies that we're not like them.) Discuss the effect this has on the reader.
- Examine the author's perspective. According to him, having a beard has pros and cons; ask the children to name them. Based on the author's attitude, ask the group if they think the author likes beards or has a beard himself.
- Ask the children to list all the food bits caught in Mr Twit's beard. From this evidence, ask: *What does Mr Twit eat for breakfast, lunch and dinner? Why does the author describe the food as 'disgusting'?* Discuss reasons why the author goes into such detail – what is his intention?
- Analyse Mr Twit's self-image. Ask: *Does he take care of himself? Why? Does he like his beard? What impression does he feel it gives? Is he correct?*
- Consider Mrs Twit's appearance. According to the author, Mrs Twit was not always ugly. Ask the group to suggest reasons for Mrs Twit's ugliness. According to the author, what makes someone lovely? Do you agree with the author?

- Hand out dictionaries and thesauruses. Let the children look up the meaning of the word 'twit' in their dictionary and then use a thesaurus to find synonyms. Encourage a discussion on when and how to use these words, and the negative effects of name-calling. What is the author trying to achieve by calling these characters 'twits'?

- Ask the children to look at the picture of Mr Twit at the beginning of Chapter 2 'Mr Twit', and point out the simile in the text ('It grew in spikes that stuck out straight like the bristles of a nailbrush.'). Then ask if it is an effective comparison. Ask them to think of their own similes for his beard: 'His beard was like…', or 'His beard was as hairy as…', or 'The hairs on his face grew out like…'.

- Examine each other's reactions. Ask the group: *Do you like Mr and Mrs Twit? Why/Why not?*

Ask the children, whenever appropriate, to revisit the text to exemplify/support their answers.

Encourage the children to read aloud to the group when referring back to the text – praise clear, confident and expressive reading.

Before the next session
Ask the children to read from Chapter 5 'The Glass Eye' to Chapter 10 'Mrs Twit Gets a Stretching'.

ASSESSMENT OPPORTUNITIES

The following bank of question prompts provides a quick and easy means of monitoring the children's comprehension skills and understanding of the text. The children's answers to a question must be supported by evidence from the text.

Understanding
- Why did Mrs Twit carry a stick?
- Give reasons why Mr Twit's beard is so dirty.
- How do we know Mrs Twit is partially blind?
- If you could interview Mrs Twit, what questions would you ask her?

Inferences
- Do you think the author has a beard? Give a reason for your answer.
- What clues suggest Mrs Twit is mean?
- In Chapter 3 'Dirty Beards', why does the narrator tell the reader to 'hold your noses, ladies and gentlemen'?

Predicting
- After reading about Mr and Mrs Twit, how do you think they treat each other and other people? Find clues in the text to support your answer.
- Will Mr and Mrs Twit change or stay the same in the story?

Main ideas
- Read the first four chapter titles. What do they tell the reader?
- In two sentences, summarise Mr and Mrs Twit.
- Identify a key sentence in Chapter 4 'Mrs Twit' that sums up the author's message to the reader.

Language, structure and presentation
- Look through the text and find words and phrases the author uses for 'beard'.
- Find synonyms in the text for the word 'horrible'.
- What is a 'tasty morsel'?
- Find the simile in Chapter 4 'Mrs Twit' that compares a person's good thoughts to sunshine.

Themes and conventions
- Why did the author choose this title for the book?
- Explain whether the book is written in first or third person narrative.
- Explain how the pictures support the text, giving examples.

SESSION AIMS

Infer characters' feelings and identify themes and conventions.

BEFORE THE SESSION

The children should have read Chapters 5 to 10 prior to the session.

READ

- Ask the children to go to the contents page and read the chapter titles from Chapter 5 'The Glass Eye' to Chapter 10 'Mrs Twit Gets a Stretching'. Have a quick group discussion to recall the story so far:
  - Summarise what happens in each chapter.
  - What are the Twits doing to each other?
  - According to Mr Twit, what is Mrs Twit suffering from?
  - Predict what will happen to Mrs Twit.
- Invite them to read Chapters 11 'Mrs Twit Goes Ballooning Up', 12 'Mrs Twit Comes Ballooning Down' and 13 'Mr Twit Gets a Horrid Shock'.

During reading

While reading the three chapters, ask the children to consider the following questions:

- What nasty idea did Mr Twit have?
- What did he hope would happen?
- Did his plan work? Why?
- If your school uses reading journals then the children should be encouraged to make notes as they read and consider each question.
- Move around the group and 'tune in' to hear individuals read aloud. Encourage and praise good expression.

After reading, ask the group to predict how Mrs Twit will get her revenge.

REVISIT AND RESPOND

Use the following discussion points to help the children think about what they have read in more depth.

Note: Since there are only 20 minutes for each session, you are advised to focus on only one or two of the elements that are listed below.

- Identify the main theme of the story. Refer to the first line of Chapters 6 'The Frog', 7 'The Wormy Spaghetti' and 8 'The Funny Walking-Stick'. Ask the children to identify the pattern of the Twits' behaviour (tit-for-tat). Ask: *Is this behaviour appropriate for adults? Why do the Twits behave so childishly? What do you think will happen next?*

- Consider values and attitudes. Ask: *Was Mr Twit fair to Mrs Twit when he cut the balloon strings? Did he intend to do it? Could he have 'overdone it'?* Ask the group if they think Mrs Twit deserved this. Some may feel yes and others no. Encourage them to express their opinions.

- Urge the group to discuss the author's intention in creating such unlikeable characters. What does he want readers to feel towards them? Ask: *Do you like anything about the characters? Have they done anything worthy?* Finally, ask whether the children care about Mr or Mrs Twit.

- Discuss humour in the text. Ask the group to identify their favourite funny part in these 'trick-playing' chapters and explain why it's funny (Roald Dahl is known for his twisted sense of humour). Ask: *What words, names and phrases does the author use to make the reader laugh?*

- Analyse Mr Twit's language. Ask the group if Mr Twit means it when he says 'We wouldn't want anything like that to happen', calls Mrs Twit 'my angel' and describes her floating away as 'a pretty sight'. Explain what sarcasm is. Sarcasm can be hurtful but also funny. Ask them to explain why it is funny in this context.

- Examine Mrs Twit's reaction. Ask: *When Mrs Twit returns from the sky, what does she do to Mr Twit? How does she feel? What does she mean by 'I'll swash you to a swizzle', 'gnash you to a gnozzle'* and 'gnosh you to a gnazzle'? Let the children give their own interpretations and, if time permits, they can invent their own nonsense threats.

- Visualise the scene. Ask the children to imagine what 'a bundle of balloons and petticoats and fiery fury' looks like. Then, get them to search Chapter 13 'Mr Twit Gets a Horrid Shock' for any other descriptions of Mrs Twit that give the reader an amusing mental image. Discuss the humour and ask if it makes them more sympathetic towards Mrs Twit.

- Analyse the text. Refer to Chapter 9 'Mrs Twit Has the Shrinks'. Ask them to identify words in italics or in capital letters. Encourage them to read parts of the chapter aloud, using the textual clues to add expression. What effect does the repetition have – should they slow down or speed up?

- Relate to the characters. Ask: *Who is worse off when being tricked? Does anyone feel sorry for Mr or Mrs Twit, in one of those tricky situations? Have you ever been tricked? Did you find it funny? How did you feel?*

Ask the children, whenever appropriate, to revisit the text to exemplify/support their answers.

Encourage the children to read aloud to the group when referring back to the text – praise clear, confident and expressive reading.

Before the next session
Ask the children to read Chapter 14 'The House, the Tree and the Monkey Cage'.

ASSESSMENT OPPORTUNITIES
The following bank of question prompts provides a quick and easy means of monitoring the children's comprehension skills and understanding of the text. The children's answers to a question must be supported by evidence from the text.

Understanding
- Did Mr Twit really 'get rid of' Mrs Twit?
- What is the historical meaning of 'stretching', and whom did it involve?
- Despite having bad qualities, what are Mr and Mrs Twit very good at doing?

Inferences
- What suggests Mrs Twit trusted Mr Twit?
- How do you know Mr Twit was happy about his wife's disappearance into the sky?
- What clues suggest that the Twits don't care about each other?

Predicting
- By the end of Chapter 13 'Mr Twit Gets a Horrid Shock', whose turn is it to play a prank?
- What kind of prank might occur next?

Main ideas
- How many tricks are described? Summarise each in a sentence.
- Why are the Twits so mean to each other?

Language, structure and presentation
- Identify the made-up words in Chapter 13 'Mr Twit Gets a Horrid Shock' and suggest their meaning. Are they verbs, nouns or adjectives?
- Identify the exclamations and the use of onomatopoeia. What effect do these have when reading the story?
- Make a list of the mean names the Twits call each other and identify any metaphors (such as 'old goat' and 'old hag').
- Give examples of alliteration from the text. How does this add to the fun of the story?
- Choose a picture and write your own caption, and then add speech bubbles.

Themes and conventions
- Explain the humour in these chapter titles: 'Mrs Twit Goes Ballooning Up' and 'Mrs Twit Comes Ballooning Down'.
- What is the story's main theme so far? (Revenge.)
- The chapter titles map the story plot, but do they spoil the story for readers? Explain the reasons for your answer.

▼ SESSION 3: KEEP OUT!

SESSION AIMS

Draw inferences (such as characters' feelings) from their actions, discuss interesting words and phrases and ask questions.

BEFORE THE SESSION

The children should have read Chapter 14 'The House, the Tree and the Monkey Cage' independently prior to the session.

READ

- Ask the children to recall Chapter 14 'The House, the Tree and the Monkey Cage'. Have a quick group discussion based on these questions:
  - How does the chapter title link to the chapter?
  - What is the purpose of this chapter?
  - Which characters are introduced?
  - Do you find anything odd or amusing about the Twits' home?
  - Do any questions arise about the house or the garden?
  - Have you learned anything new about the Twits?
- Read Chapters 15 'Hugtight Sticky Glue' and 16 'Four Sticky Little Boys'.

During reading

- Consider the punctuation, capitalisation, italics, exclamations and dashes used to add emphasis and expression.
- Notice how the pictures support the story.
- If your school uses reading journals then the children should be encouraged to make notes as they read and consider each question.
- Move around the group and 'tune in' to hear individuals read aloud. Encourage and praise good expression.
- When they have finished reading, ask the children if they think the little boys got what they deserved.

REVISIT AND RESPOND

Use the following discussion points to help the children think about what they have read in more depth.

Note: Since there are only 20 minutes for each session, you are advised to focus on only one or two of the elements that are listed below.

- Focus on the setting. Refer to the picture of the Twits' house in Chapter 14 'The House, the Tree and the Monkey Cage'. Ask: *What does the author compare it to?* Encourage the group to imagine what it's like inside. Ask: *Would you like to live here? Why?* Then switch focus to the garden. Ask: *How would you describe it? Does anything in it look interesting or fun?*

- Draw the children's attention to how the author addresses the reader directly ('And what do you think of that ghastly garden?'). Ask: *What does the author think about the garden? Does his opinion affect that of the reader?* Discuss the possibility that there might be another opinion about the garden. Ask: *How does Mrs Twit feel about the garden?*

- Discuss the humour in the statement 'Mr Twit was good at catching birds'. Consider his method of bird-catching. Ask: *Did the birds stand a chance? Was it fair? Why did he use this method? Did it require any skill? In what way was he 'good' at it?*

- Consider values and attitudes. Ask: *Do you think it's acceptable to catch birds and eat them? Why is Mr Twit's behaviour unacceptable? Did he care how he caught them? Can you suggest a better approach?*

- Consider Mr Twit's state of mind. Draw the children's attention to the picture above Chapter 15's title 'Hugtight Sticky Glue', and ask them to describe Mr Twit's expression. Ask: *What might Mr Twit be thinking? What are his intentions? How does his mood change when the plan fails in the next chapter?*

- Explore motives and consequences. Ask the children to explain why the boys ventured into the garden. The author writes 'There's nothing wrong with that'. Ask: *Do you agree with the author or do you think they were trespassing? Was Mr Twit justified in getting angry?*

- Invite the children to imagine how the boys felt, stuck in the tree. Ask: *Why were they so terrified of Mr Twit? How did they escape?* Get the children to look at the picture of them running away. Ask: *What do you notice in the picture? Can you tell how they feel about getting free?* Ask the children what they think happened when the boys got home.

- Analyse the characters' attitudes. Ask: *What evidence suggests the Twits dislike animals and children? Why do you think they don't like them?*

Ask the children, whenever appropriate, to revisit the text to exemplify/support their answers.

Encourage the children to read aloud to the group when referring back to the text – praise clear, confident and expressive reading.

Before the next session
Ask the children to read Chapter 17 'The Great Upside Down Monkey Circus' and Chapter 18 'The Roly-Poly Bird to the Rescue'.

ASSESSMENT OPPORTUNITIES

The following bank of question prompts provides a quick and easy means of monitoring the children's comprehension skills and understanding of the text. The children's answers to a question must be supported by evidence from the text.

Understanding
- What purpose does Mr Twit believe windows have? Name some others.

- Why does Mrs Twit like to grow spiky and stinging things in her garden?

- What sort of birds did Mr Twit catch for his pie? Why didn't he care which birds went into the pie?

- What is a 'wretched' bird? Explain the phrase in the context of the story.

- Why did the little boys go into the Twits' garden?

Inferences
- Would you like to eat Mrs Twit's pie? Give a reason for your answer.

- Is Mrs Twit really good at growing things?

- Why do you think the monkeys are in a cage in the garden?

Predicting
- What clues suggest the monkeys will be part of the story?

- Do you think Mr Twit intended to eat the little boys? What might have happened if he'd caught them?

- Once the little boys escaped, where do you think they ran to?

- Do you think the boys ever returned to the Twits' garden?

Main ideas
- Find one word in the text that describes the house and one that describes the garden.

- Does Mr Twit want visitors? What sign do you think Mr Twit should put up in his garden?

Language, structure and presentation
- Why is 'HUGTIGHT' written in capital letters?

- Make up your own glue names using compound words, such as 'Stickfast' or 'Foreverglue'.

- Identify and explain the expression in the sentence 'Who wants every Tom, Dick and Harry peeping in to see what you're doing?'.

- In what way do the pictures add to the story?

Themes and conventions
- There is a lot of humour in this story. Explain the humour in the picture of Mr Twit's bird pie at the end of Chapter 15 'Hugtight Sticky Glue'.

- Explain the word 'cruelty' in the context of these chapters.

SESSION 4: MONKEY BUSINESS

SESSION AIMS

Predict what might happen from details stated, draw inferences and consider how language contributes to meaning.

BEFORE THE SESSION

The children should have read Chapters 17 'The Great Upside Down Monkey Circus' and 18 'The Roly-Poly Bird to the Rescue' independently prior to the session.

READ

- Have a quick recall session using the following questions to guide the discussion:
  - Where do the monkeys live and why?
  - What is their problem?
  - Who do the monkeys ask to help them?
- Ask the children to look at the next two chapter headings and predict what will happen before reading both chapters.

During reading

- Check their understanding by asking the following:
  - Do the titles of the chapters spoil the reading of the story?
  - Why is there no bird pie for Mr Twit?
- If your school uses reading journals then the children should be encouraged to make notes as they read and consider each question.
- Move around the group and 'tune in' to hear individuals read aloud. Encourage and praise good expression.
- Knowing what Mr Twit is like, ask the children: *How is he likely to react to not getting what he wants?*

REVISIT AND RESPOND

Use the following discussion points to help the children think about what they have read in more depth.

Note: Since there are only 20 minutes for each session, you are advised to focus on only one or two of the elements that are listed below.

- In the story, we learn that Mr and Mrs Twit used to work in a circus. Ask: *What did they do? Do you think they were good at their job? Why?* Invite the group to discuss whether the Twits would do well as circus trainers today and give reasons.
- Consider values and attitudes. Ask: *How does Mr Twit treat the monkeys? What does he do to them? Why?* Ask the children how they feel about keeping animals in cages. Encourage them to suggest better ways to look after animals in captivity.
- Examine Mr Twit's dreams for the future. Ask: *What does Mr Twit want to do? Is it surprising to find out that he has plans for the future?* Ask the group to decide if they are inspired by Mr Twit's dream, giving reasons for their answer. Compare Mr Twit's dream with Muggle-Wump's hopes for the future. Encourage the children to predict who will realise their dreams in this story.
- Look at how the animals communicate. Ask: *Why were the monkeys unable to communicate with the English birds? Why did they need the Roly-Poly Bird? Who spoke which language?* Invite the group to compare the animals' communication to that of the Twits – are they rude like the Twits? Let them give examples. Discuss what message the author is trying to convey.
- Focus on the Roly-Poly Bird. Ask: *What was the Roly-Poly Bird doing in England? Is it a real or imaginary bird? How does the author describe the bird? Does the picture in Chapter 18 'The Roly-Poly Bird to the Rescue' match the description or did you visualise something else?* Invite the children to choose their own adjectives to describe its appearance.

- Focus on the monkey family. Ask the children to think about the kind of family the Muggle-Wump monkeys are. The children should scan through the chapters to pick up clues and make notes. Share ideas about the monkey family's size, their activities, values, hopes and dreams. Invite the children to compare the monkey family to the Twits family. Ask: *Which family would you prefer to meet and why?*

- Analyse the song of the Roly-Poly Bird. Ask the children to explain what the Roly-Poly Bird did to prevent the birds from getting stuck in the tree. Let them read the song aloud with expression, emphasising the rhythm. Ask: *Was the song effective? How do you know?* Encourage the children to think up a third verse of the song, to continue the story.

- Decide what is fact and what is fiction. Ask the children to identify the parts of the story that could be real and the parts that are imaginary (monkeys are real, but monkeys that speak a human language are not). Ask: *What could be real and what is definitely fiction?*

Ask the children, whenever appropriate, to revisit the text to exemplify/support their answers.

Encourage the children to read aloud to the group when referring back to the text – praise clear, confident and expressive reading.

ASSESSMENT OPPORTUNITIES

The following bank of question prompts provides a quick and easy means of monitoring the children's comprehension skills and understanding of the text. The children's answers to a question must be supported by evidence from the text.

Understanding
- Why did the monkeys hate performing tricks for Mr Twit?
- The monkeys tried to warn the birds about the glue on the tree but the birds didn't listen. Why?
- Why did the birds respond to the Roly-Poly Bird?

Inferences
- How can you tell the monkeys were surprised to see the Roly-Poly Bird?
- What clues suggest that the Roly-Poly Bird travelled a lot?
- Does the Roly-Poly Bird sound friendly? Give examples to back up your answer.
- How do you know the Roly-Poly Bird can speak many languages?

Predicting
- How do the chapter titles alert the reader about what's to come?
- Do you think the Roly-Poly Bird's job is over? Explain your answer.
- Read Chapter 21's title, 'Mr and Mrs Twit Go Off to Buy Guns', and predict how the Twits are planning to solve the problem of no birds for their pie.

Main ideas
- Identify the antagonists (villains) and protagonists (heroes).
- Summarise the problems that the monkeys must solve.
- Summarise the problems that the Twits must solve.

Language, structure and presentation
- What word class (part of speech) is 'Muggle-Wump'?
- Why is 'GREAT UPSIDE DOWN MONKEY CIRCUS' written in capitals?
- Why is 'The Big Dead Tree' written with capital letters on each initial letter?
- Identify examples of alliteration in the text and explain why it is used.

Themes and conventions
- Consider the length of Chapter 19 'No Bird Pie for Mr Twit'. Why did the author make it so short? What is the effect of such a short chapter?
- Explain the expression 'as free as a bird' in the context of this story.
- How is the revenge theme continued in these chapters?

▼ SESSION 5: MAKING PLANS

SESSION AIMS

Discuss interesting words and phrases, identify main ideas and draw inferences.

BEFORE THE SESSION

The children should have read Chapters 21 'Mr and Mrs Twit Go Off to Buy Guns' and 22 'Muggle-Wump Has an Idea' independently prior to the session.

READ

- Involve the group in a quick recap session, discussing the following questions:
  - Where did the Twits go? Why?
  - How did the monkeys escape from their cage?
  - What was Muggle-Wump's idea?
- Ask the children how they would describe the mood among the animals. What has changed?
- Invite the children to now read the next three chapters.

During reading

- Ask the children to keep the following questions in mind:
  - Who helped Muggle-Wump?
  - Did Muggle-Wump know how his plan would turn out?
  - What will happen next?
- If your school uses reading journals then the children should be encouraged to make notes as they read and consider each question.
- Move around the group and 'tune in' to hear individuals read aloud. Encourage and praise good expression.
- Ask the children to explain why Muggle-Wump is doing this, and where he got his idea from.

REVISIT AND RESPOND

Use the following discussion points to help the children think about what they have read in more depth.

Note: Since there are only 20 minutes for each session, you are advised to focus on only one or two of the elements that are listed below.

- Compare both plans. Ask the children to identify the Twits' problem and their plan of action and then Muggle-Wump's problem and plan of action. Ask: *Which idea was more realistic? Which one do you think will succeed? Why?*
- Explain Mr Twit's behaviour. Why was he happy to announce his 'great idea' in front of the monkeys instead of keeping it a secret? As he thinks they cannot understand him, explain why Mr Twit expects the monkeys to listen to him later on when he orders them about. Ask: *What tone of voice does he use to give orders? Why do the monkeys obey?*
- Look at the name-calling in Chapter 24 'The Carpet Goes on the Ceiling'. Ask the group to identify who calls whom what. Discuss the meaning of the names. Ask: *Are the animals being nasty? Compare this to how the Twits speak to each other. How is it different?*
- Ask the children to identify all those who help Muggle-Wump carry out his plan of action. Ask: *Could he have done it on his own? What job did everyone have? Who gave the orders? Was it an easy job?* Explain how this is a good example of the value of teamwork. Find out how the children feel about working together and let them express what they like or dislike about it. When does it work best?
- Consider the language. Ask the children to skim the text and identify repetition of words and phrases, such as 'Hurry up, hurry up!' and 'Come on, come on!'. Ask: *What effect does this repetition have on the pace and mood of the story?*
- Discuss values and attitudes. Ask: *Do you think Muggle-Wump was right to do as he did, yelling at everyone and risking their freedom when they could have run away?* Encourage suggestions.

- Focus the group's attention on the timing of the events in the story. The ideas of both Mr Twit and Muggle-Wump play out at the same time. Ask: *How does it contribute to a build-up of suspension and excitement?*

- Focus on the language. The Twits describe the birds as 'filthy feathery frumps', Muggle-Wump describes the Twits as 'frumptious freaks' and the Roly-Poly Bird describes the Twits as 'maggoty old monsters'. Invite the children to identify the figure of speech (alliteration) and explain its effect. Ask: *Does it add to the humour?*

Ask the children, whenever appropriate, to revisit the text to exemplify/support their answers.

Encourage the children to read aloud to the group when referring back to the text – praise clear, confident and expressive reading.

ASSESSMENT OPPORTUNITIES

The following bank of question prompts provides a quick and easy means of monitoring the children's comprehension skills and understanding of the text. The children's answers to a question must be supported by evidence from the text.

Understanding

- Why did Mrs Twit agree to Mr Twit's plan? What did she want him to avoid?

- Mrs Twit locked the house and hid the key. How did the monkeys get into the house?

- Why did the Roly-Poly Bird ask Muggle-Wump not to mention Bird Pie?

Inferences

- Is there evidence to suggest that Muggle-Wump had planned his escape for a while, or was it a spontaneous idea?

- How do we know that Muggle-Wump's children had other ideas of what to do when they got out of the cage?

- Compare the birds that helped Muggle-Wump to the list of birds in Mrs Twit's bird pie. What do you notice?

- How do you know the monkeys are in a hurry to carry out the plan?

Predicting

- How would the story plot change if the monkeys had decided to simply run away?

- How would the plot change if the Twits had arrived home early?

- What will happen when the Twits arrive home?

Main ideas

- Compare Mr and Mrs Twit's house to the monkey cage. Identify the common element.

- The monkeys break free but choose not to run away immediately. Why?

Language, structure and presentation

- Find a word in the text that sums up Muggle-Wump's idea.

- What does the expression 'hooting with laughter' mean?

- Why is this expression funny: 'I'll wipe that silly laugh off your beaks!'?

- Explain the simile: he was 'like a demon hopping round the room'. To whom did it refer?

- Identify all the words used for 'said' in Chapter 21 'Mr and Mrs Twit Go Off to Buy Guns'. What do these words indicate about Mr Twit's mood and behaviour?

Themes and conventions

- What is Muggle-Wump's reason for wanting to turn the Twits upside down? Find a sentence that supports your answer.

- Explain the expression 'Many hands make light work' in the context of these chapters.

- Since the monkeys have escaped, are they now free? What would help them to feel completely free?

▼ SESSION 6: REVENGE

SESSION AIMS

Identify and discuss themes and conventions and consider how language, structure and presentation contribute to meaning.

BEFORE THE SESSION

The children should have read Chapter 26 'The Ravens Swoop Over' independently prior to the session.

READ

- Ask the children to recall the chapter read independently. Have a quick recall session using the following questions:
  - How did the monkeys know the Twits had returned?
  - What did the Twits have with them?
  - What did the ravens do?
- Ask the children if they can predict why the ravens did this.
- Then read as a group the final three chapters.

During reading

- While reading, ask the children to keep the following questions in mind:
  - How did the Twits react at what they saw when they entered the living room?
  - Where did the monkeys go?
  - What plan did the Roly-Poly Bird suggest?
  - What happened to the Twits?
- If your school uses reading journals then the children should be encouraged to make notes as they read and consider each question.
- Move around the group and 'tune in' to hear individuals read aloud. Encourage and praise good expression.
- Discuss whether the children enjoyed the end of the story. Ask: *Was it a satisfactory ending? Could there have been another possible outcome?*

REVISIT AND RESPOND

Use the following discussion points to help the children think about what they have read in more depth.

Note: Since there are only 20 minutes for each session, you are advised to focus on only one or two of the elements that are listed below.

- In Chapter 26 'The Ravens Swoop Over' ask the children to find evidence to suggest that when Mr and Mrs Twit returned, they had no idea what the monkeys had been up to. Ask the children to explain Mr Twit's assumption about the monkeys, and the humour in Mrs Twit's statement: 'They're too stupid to do anything else'.
- Analyse Mr Twit's moody personality. Invite the children to describe the Twits' mood when they returned from town. Ask: *Why were they so cheerful? How did Mr Twit react to the birds? What did he threaten to do to them?* Discuss how his mood changed from one minute to the next.
- Give the children time to look at the picture of the upside-down living room. Ask them what effect the double-page spread has. Let them turn the book 'upside down' to view the room and identify all the objects, then ask: *Do you think the monkeys did a good job? How does it feel to turn the book upside down?* Explain why Mrs Twit felt 'giddy'.
- Analyse the Twits' reaction. When the Twits walked into the living room, they quickly decided what the problem was without finding out the facts. Ask the children to think of questions the Twits should have asked before they drew their own conclusions.
- Refer the children to the picture of the Twits on their heads. Ask: *Do you find it funny? Does it make you feel sorry for them? Why?* Invite the children to imagine and describe how the animals reacted when they saw this sight. Discuss reasons why the author left this to our imagination.
- Focus on setting. Once the monkeys knew they were safe, where did they go? Compare their new home to their old one.

- Analyse character development. Ask the children to think about how each character's situation changed in the story. Then invite them to decide if the characters themselves changed or didn't change. Ask: *Who do you feel you know the best by the end of the story?*

- Consider the characters' roles. Why do most of the characters in the story have important roles? Ask the children who the main character or characters are. Which character is their favourite and why?

- Focus on the final chapter, Chapter 29 'The Twits Get the Shrinks'. Invite the children to explain what happened to the Twits in the end and link it to the trick Mr Twit played on Mrs Twit earlier in the story. Ask: *How does it fit the story's main theme of revenge?* Discuss issues around the theme of revenge by asking: *Where did it start? Do you think the monkeys were justified? Is revenge always a satisfactory solution?*

- Discuss the humour in the final chapters. The author deals with a serious event (the death of Mr and Mrs Twit) in a humorous way. Ask the children to identify the serious aspect and then explain what makes it funny. Discuss the author's intention in dealing with this serious event in a humorous way.

Ask the children, whenever appropriate, to revisit the text to exemplify/support their answers.

Encourage the children to read aloud to the group when referring back to the text – praise clear, confident and expressive reading.

ASSESSMENT OPPORTUNITIES

The following bank of question prompts provides a quick and easy means of monitoring the children's comprehension skills and understanding of the text. The children's answers to a question must be supported by evidence from the text.

Understanding
- In what order did the furniture go up on the ceiling?
- How did Muggle-Wump know that the glue would work? How did he describe it?
- Why did Muggle-Wump use ravens to smear glue on to the top of Mr and Mrs Twit's heads? Why not ask the other birds?

Inferences
- How do you know the monkeys wanted to see what happened to the Twits when they entered the house?
- What clues suggest the Twits died?

Predicting
- What do you think would have happened if the Twits had arrived home and worked out they had been fooled?
- What else could the animals have done, without being mean, to teach the Twits a lesson?

Main ideas
- Compare Mr Twit and Muggle-Wump. Identify similarities and differences between them.
- Make a list of all the tricks in the story and compare the first one with the final one. Explain how things got out of hand. What lesson can we learn?

Language, structure and presentation
- Explain what a 'dollop' of sticky glue is. Is 'dollop' a real word?
- Identify the use of punctuation, italics, capital letters and ellipses in the final chapter. Explain why the author uses them.

Themes and conventions
- Summarise the story plot and then describe its climax.
- Explain the expression 'what goes around comes around' in the context of the story.

▼ SESSION 1: THE COMING OF THE IRON MAN

SESSION AIMS

Consider the character of the Iron Man and identify any characteristics of fairy tale in the story and devices used by the author that add quality.

READ

- Explain to the children that the story they are about to read has been described as 'a modern fairy tale'. Ask: *Thinking of fairy tales you know, what are the common ingredients of a fairy tale?* They may suggest good and evil characters, magic of some kind, unexpected twists, being set in a world that is familiar yet unfamiliar. Ask them to keep these ingredients in mind as they read *The Iron Man,* to see if they agree that it could be described as a fairy tale.

- Invite them to consider the title of the book. What do they expect the story to be about? Some may suggest a robot. Ask if their ideas match what they would expect of a fairy tale. Remind them that this is a *modern* fairy tale. Does this alter their opinion?

During reading

- Ask the children to read Chapter 1 independently, keeping in mind the fairy tale ideas you have discussed.

- When they have finished reading, invite the children to comment on any fairy tale elements they noticed.

- If your school uses reading journals then the children should be encouraged to make notes as they read and consider each question.

- Move around the group and 'tune in' to hear individuals read aloud. Encourage and praise good expression.

REVISIT AND RESPOND

Use the following discussion points to help the children think about what they have read in more depth.

Note: Since there are only 20 minutes for each session, you are advised to focus on only one or two of the elements that are listed below.

- Invite the children to share their first impressions of the Iron Man. Is he a good or bad character? What are the reasons for their opinions? How would they feel if they had seen what happened to him?

- Ask the children to think about the information we are given about the Iron Man, and the questions it raises. On the first page we are told that nobody knows how far he had walked, where he had come from or how he was made. Later in the chapter they might ask themselves: *How does he know how to put himself back together? How can he breathe underwater?* Can the children suggest answers for some of these unknown questions?

- Ask the children to skim-read the first two or three pages, taking note of the length of the sentences. Afterwards, ask what they found. They will probably notice that there are many very short sentences. Ask them why they think Ted Hughes has deliberately used this device; for example, it affects the way we read the text, slowing us down to give more emphasis to what we are reading; it makes it easier to understand. Explain that Ted Hughes was mostly known as a poet and he uses many poetic devices in his story writing, such as choosing words carefully and not using unnecessary words.

- Ask the children to skim-read the first two or three pages, looking for examples of repetition (for example, in the following phrases: 'Nobody knows'; 'slowly turned'; 'He swayed'; 'right foot'; 'CRASH!'; 'His... fell off', and so on). Ask: *What does this deliberate repetition add to the writing?* Agree that it provides emphasis and rhythm and is one of the ingredients often found in the telling of fairy tales.

Ask the children, whenever appropriate, to revisit the text to exemplify/support their answers.

Encourage the children to read aloud to the group when referring back to the text – praise clear, confident and expressive reading.

Before the next session
Ask the children to read Chapter 2 up to, and including, the paragraph beginning 'At last they put up a little notice…'. Ask them to think about how the plot develops. Is it what they expected?

ASSESSMENT OPPORTUNITIES
The following bank of question prompts provides a quick and easy means of monitoring the children's comprehension skills and understanding of the text. The children's answers to a question must be supported by evidence from the text.

Understanding
- What did 'nobody know' about the Iron Man?
- What does Ted Hughes compare the Iron Man's eyes to?
- How did the Iron Man's head move?
- How big was the Iron Man's head?
- What shape was the Iron Man's head?
- What sounds were there after the Iron Man fell off the cliff onto the rocky beach?
- What do the gulls have that the Iron Man is looking for?
- What did the gulls think the Iron Man's eye was?
- What did the gulls think the Iron Man's hand was?
- What thing belonging to the Iron Man could the seagulls and their chicks not eat?

Inferences
- Why was it important for the Iron Man to begin putting himself back together starting with an eye and a hand?
- How do we know that the Iron Man is bigger than a person?
- Do you think the Iron Man fell from the cliff or stepped off deliberately? Explain your reasons.
- Why do you think the Iron Man had never seen the sea before?

- Why did no one know that the Iron Man had fallen from the cliff?
- What do the different colours of the Iron Man's eyes suggest to you?
- How do you think the Iron Man knew how to put himself back together?
- Why do you think the Iron Man walked into the sea?

Predicting
- What do you think will happen next? Will the story continue underwater, or somewhere else?
- We know that the Iron Man's ear is still on the ledge near the seagulls. Do you think this will be important later in the story? Explain why you think it will or will not.

Main ideas
- What does the presence of the seagulls add to the story?
- How is the author trying to make you feel about the Iron Man in this opening chapter?

Language, structure and presentation
- Scan the text and list some words and phrases used to describe the Iron Man.
- Which phrase tells us that it is night time?
- Find the meanings of the words 'brink' and 'immense' in a dictionary.

Themes and conventions
- Why do you think questions are used at the beginning of the story?

▼ SESSION 2: THE RETURN OF THE IRON MAN

SESSION AIMS

Consider the character of Hogarth and his reactions to events.

BEFORE THE SESSION

The children should have read part of Chapter 2, up to and including the paragraph beginning 'At last they put up a little notice…'.

READ

- Ask the children at what point in their reading of Chapter 2 did they realise that the Iron Man had come back? What was it in the writing that told them? If they had been Hogarth, would they have reacted in the same way as him and run away?

- Did the children have some idea of how the story would continue? Did they expect the Iron Man to come back? Why?

- We are told that Hogarth's father and one of the farmers believed Hogarth's story. Why do the children think we needed to be told this? What usually happens in stories when a child tells an adult about something unusual and unexpected?

- Invite the children to suggest what the night-time setting of the chapter opening adds to the story, finding examples in the text to support their ideas.

- Do the children think the farmers' plan to dig a hole was a good idea? Ask them to explain their opinions. What else might the farmers have done?

During reading

- Ask the children to read on to the end of Chapter 2, thinking about Hogarth's actions.

- If your school uses reading journals then the children should be encouraged to make notes as they read and consider each question.

- Move around the group and 'tune in' to hear individuals read aloud. Encourage and praise good expression.

REVISIT AND RESPOND

Use the following discussion points to help the children think about what they have read in more depth.

Note: Since there are only 20 minutes for each session, you are advised to focus on only one or two of the elements that are listed below.

- Ask the children to suggest why it was a long time before the Iron Man returned. Where had he been? What had he been doing? Why did he come back at all?

- Ask the children to think about Hogarth. What are their feelings about him? What is their opinion of what he did in this chapter (set out to capture a fox with a dead hen, lured the Iron Man into the pit, told everyone what he had done, then felt sorry and guilty at the end)?

- Invite the children to think about the Iron Man and their feelings towards him. Do they feel the same as they did when they first encountered him in Chapter 1? Is he a scary creature? Is he clever? Would they be afraid of him? Can they suggest why he is eating all the metal he can find? Do they think he would eat other things?

- If the story had been set in a city instead of the countryside, what metal objects would the Iron Man have found to eat?

- Invite the children to select any short section from Chapter 2 that they particularly enjoyed reading, giving reasons for their choice.

Ask the children, whenever appropriate, to revisit the text to exemplify/support their answers.

Encourage the children to read aloud to the group when referring back to the text – praise clear, confident and expressive reading.

Before the next session

Ask the children to revisit Chapters 1 and 2, listing words and phrases used to describe the Iron Man. Ask them to use these as prompts to draw their own annotated drawing of the Iron Man, to bring with them to the next session. (Explain that this is what the book's illustrator would have done, but that the children's drawings are their own interpretations.)

ASSESSMENT OPPORTUNITIES

The following bank of question prompts provides a quick and easy means of monitoring the children's comprehension skills and understanding of the text. The children's answers to a question must be supported by evidence from the text.

Understanding

- What did Hogarth plan to catch in the trap? What did he use as bait?
- What did Hogarth hear as he waited in the tree to see if his plan had worked?
- What stopped the fox from stepping into Hogarth's trap?
- What did Hogarth think he must do when he first saw the Iron Man again?
- Why would the Iron Man not fall into the trap while he was eating the barbed-wire fence?
- What did Hogarth do with his knife and a nail?
- What was the farmers' reaction when they saw the Iron Man in the pit?
- Why could the Iron Man not get out of the pit?
- What did the farmers do when the Iron Man was in the pit?

Inferences

- What do you think Hogarth thought when he saw the Iron Man returning?
- Why do you think Hogarth had a knife and a nail in his pocket? What effect did this have on the Iron Man?
- How do you think Hogarth felt when the Iron Man fell into the pit?

- What does the colour-changing of the Iron Man's eyes when he was in the pit tell us about his mood?
- What do you think the farmers thought of Hogarth when he lured the Iron Man into the pit? How would Hogarth's father have felt?
- Why did the farmers go to and fro over the mound of earth?
- How does the author show us that Hogarth is quite a clever boy?

Predicting

- Have we now seen the end of the Iron Man? What do you think will happen next? Will he escape from the pit, will other iron men come looking for him, or something else?

Main ideas

- Explain why you think Hogarth felt sorry and guilty that the Iron Man had been buried.
- What are your feelings about the Iron Man? Have they changed since Chapter 1, or are they the same? Give your reasons.

Language, structure and presentation

- What did the Iron Man eat that was 'like spaghetti'?
- What effect does the repeated use of 'Clink, Clink, Clink' have in Chapter 2?
- What were the 'two deep red headlamps' that Hogarth saw in the pit?
- What sounded like 'a big lorry grinding its gears on a steep hill'? Why is this a good description?
- What words would you use to describe Hogarth?

SESSION 3: WHAT'S TO BE DONE?

SESSION AIMS

Consider the reactions of different characters to the Iron Man and question the children's opinions of the Iron Man and Hogarth.

BEFORE THE SESSION

The children should have re-read Chapters 1 and 2, and brought their drawings of the Iron Man with them to this session.

READ

- Invite the children to share their interpretations of the Iron Man in visual form, comparing them and identifying the parts of the text that informed their drawings. Ask them to discuss:
  - How alike or different are the drawings?
  - How have the descriptions helped them to create their drawings?
  - Do they enable us as readers to create a picture in our minds of what the author was describing?
- Ask them to point out any sections of text that they found particularly effective in describing the Iron Man. The children were asked to annotate their illustrations – did any of them choose to include the noises the Iron Man makes or the sizes and shapes of the various parts of his body, such as a single bed or headlamps?

During reading
- Ask the children to read Chapter 3 in this session, noting the ways in which different characters react to the Iron Man.
- If your school uses reading journals then the children should be encouraged to make notes as they read and consider each question.
- Move around the group and 'tune in' to hear individuals read aloud. Encourage and praise good expression.

REVISIT AND RESPOND

Use the following discussion points to help the children think about what they have read in more depth.

Note: Since there are only 20 minutes for each session, you are advised to focus on only one or two of the elements that are listed below.

- Did the children expect the Iron Man to return? Why? We know that he stayed under the sea for quite some time; he has now stayed buried under the earth for at least several months. Ask: *Why do you think the Iron Man doesn't return for long periods of time? How can he survive buried under the ground? Does he need to breathe like humans do?*
- Invite the children to share their observations on how the various characters reacted to the Iron Man's return (the family having a picnic, the farmers, the villagers and Hogarth). Can they suggest why Hogarth seemed unafraid?
- In Chapter 3 Hogarth speaks to the Iron Man, but we haven't heard the giant man speak at all. Why would Hogarth expect the Iron Man to understand him? How do we know that he does? If he did speak, what language do the children think he would speak – after all, we are told at the start that nobody knew where he came from? What would his voice sound like?
- Ask the children to suggest why the farmers agreed to follow Hogarth's plan before they contacted the Army. What might he have said to persuade them? How do the children feel about adults allowing a boy to be the one to approach the Iron Man?
- Ask the children to find the paragraph beginning 'They could not believe their eyes', noting the sentence length. Ask: *Why has Ted Hughes used several short sentences here?* Agree that they add pace and effect to the action.

Ask the children, whenever appropriate, to revisit the text to exemplify/support their answers.

Encourage the children to read aloud to the group when referring back to the text – praise clear, confident and expressive reading.

Before the next session

Ask the children to create a six-frame comic strip of the key events in Chapter 3, including captions.

ASSESSMENT OPPORTUNITIES

The following bank of question prompts provides a quick and easy means of monitoring the children's comprehension skills and understanding of the text. The children's answers to a question must be supported by evidence from the text.

Understanding

- How do we know that the Iron Man had been under the mound of earth for a long time?
- Why did the family go to the top of the hill?
- What was the first unexpected thing to happen as the family had their picnic?
- What did the mother say had probably caused the ground to shake?
- What happened to the family's picnic food and tablecloth?
- What caused the ground to open up?
- What did the family do when the ground opened up?
- What was the farmers' first reaction to the return of the Iron Man?
- What did the farmers decide to do when the Iron Man returned?
- What did the Iron Man do when he escaped from the hill?
- What was the deal Hogarth offered the Iron Man?
- What did the villagers do when they saw the Iron Man?
- Where did Hogarth lead the Iron Man to?
- Name at least three things the Iron Man could eat at the scrap-metal yard.
- What did the Iron Man eat that was better than any spaghetti?
- What colour did the Iron Man's eyes become when he was happy?
- What effect did the new diet have on the Iron Man's body?

Inferences

- How do we know that not everyone knew about the Iron Man being buried under the hill?
- Why do you think the Iron Man was under the ground for such a long time?
- Do you think an earthquake in Japan could cause events in a far-distant country?
- How do you think the family felt when the crack opened up in the ground?
- Why did the farmers not carry out their plan to contact the Army?
- How do you think the Iron Man was able to get out?
- Why was the Iron Man getting rusty?
- How did Hogarth know that the Iron Man had heard him knock the horseshoe against a stone?
- How do we know the Iron Man understood English?
- How do we know the farmers trusted Hogarth?

Predicting

- The chapter ends happily. What do you think might happen next in the story?

Main ideas

- What do you think the farmers thought about Hogarth after his plan had worked?
- What is your opinion of the Iron Man after reading this chapter? Has it changed? If so, why?

▼ SESSION 4: THE SPACE-BEING AND THE IRON MAN

SESSION AIMS

Consider how Ted Hughes has built the plot, introducing unexpected events to carry it forward.

BEFORE THE SESSION

The children should have created a comic strip of the key events in Chapter 3.

READ

- Invite the children to share their comic strips of the key events in Chapter 3. Did they all choose the same six events to illustrate and caption? How did they decide what to include? Did any of the children include speech bubbles? How easy was it to condense a whole chapter into six separate sections? Did it help that they had already drawn their version of the Iron Man?

- Invite the children to suggest what might happen in the next chapter, following the happy ending of Chapter 3. Will the Iron Man become part of the community? Will they find a way for him to help the farmers? Will he run out of food? Or something else?

During reading

- Ask the children to read Chapter 4 in this session. Before they begin reading, look together at the title of Chapter 4 – 'The Space-Being and the Iron Man'. What does this make them think will happen next?

- Invite them to read the first short paragraph, then ask: *What kind of emotion is created by the words 'Round eyes, busy mouths, frightened voices'? Does this suggest the chapter will be happy, exciting, tense, scary or something else?*

- As they continue to read the chapter, ask them to think about the events described, working out how they might link them to what they have read so far.

- If your school uses reading journals then the children should be encouraged to make notes as they read and consider each question.

- Move around the group and 'tune in' to hear individuals read aloud. Encourage and praise good expression.

REVISIT AND RESPOND

Use the following discussion points to help the children think about what they have read in more depth.

Note: Since there are only 20 minutes for each session, you are advised to focus on only one or two of the elements that are listed below.

- Were the children surprised by the turn of events in this chapter? Why do they think the focus suddenly changed from the Iron Man to something entirely different? For example: if the story had ended with the previous chapter, it would have been very short; this next part of the story gives an opportunity for more excitement and unexpected events, and it may be something that is going to link with the Iron Man in the following chapter.

- Remind the children that they considered the story as a 'modern fairy tale' when they first started reading. What observations can they make now about that? For example, the two unlikely events of the Iron Man himself and now the Space-Being arriving can fit into the idea of a fairy tale rather than a normal contemporary narrative.

- Ask the children to skim the text and look for where capitals have been used for words such as 'BIGGER', 'GREW', and 'NEARER'. Ask: *What effect does it have on the way you read these words? Is it a useful and successful device? What does it add to the telling of the story? How does it help you to imagine what is being described?*

- Invite the children to read the three short sentences beginning with 'Faster'. Ask them to comment on why the word has been repeated in this way, and why the sentences are so short.

- What do they think the Iron Man's great idea might be? We are told he will 'go out, as the champion of the earth against this monster from space'. Can they think of how he might do that?

Ask the children, whenever appropriate, to revisit the text to exemplify/support their answers.

Encourage the children to read aloud to the group when referring back to the text – praise clear, confident and expressive reading.

Before the next session
Ask the children to re-read Chapter 4, noting interesting and effective uses of language – for example, sentence length, use of description, vocabulary choice, how the structure creates tension, and so on.

ASSESSMENT OPPORTUNITIES
The following bank of question prompts provides a quick and easy means of monitoring the children's comprehension skills and understanding of the text. The children's answers to a question must be supported by evidence from the text.

Understanding
• Which constellation had the star been part of? What shape was the constellation?
• How did the star change?
• What did people expect to happen as the star got closer to earth?
• What did the astronomers think might be flying out of the centre of the star?
• What colour was the star?
• What did the astronomers use to follow what was happening in the sky?
• Where did the space-bat-angel-dragon land?
• What effect on other parts of the world did the landing of the space-bat-angel-dragon have?
• What effect did the space-bat-angel-dragon's landing have on Australia?
• Where was the only light to be found after the space-bat-angel-dragon landed on Australia?
• How big was the space-bat-angel-dragon's head?
• What did the space-bat-angel-dragon want to eat?
• How big was the space-bat-angel-dragon's stomach?

• What was the space-bat-angel-dragon's reaction after it had been attacked by the bombs and missiles?
• How long did the space-bat-angel-dragon give the people of the earth to prepare its first meal?

Inferences
• What do you think people hoped for when the star stopped growing or getting nearer?
• In the several days that it took the space-bat-angel-dragon to reach earth, what do you think the people were doing and thinking?
• Why did the space-bat-angel-dragon's landing on Australia not kill everyone?
• Why did the people of the earth decide that they would not feed the space-bat-angel-dragon?
• How do we know that Hogarth no longer saw the Iron Man as dangerous?
• How do we know that the Iron Man could speak the same language as Hogarth?

Predicting
• How do you think the Iron Man will fight the space-bat-angel-dragon?

Main ideas
• Why do you think Hogarth thought the Iron Man would be able to do something about the space-bat-angel-dragon?

Language, structure and presentation
• Look up the word 'astronomers' in a dictionary and explain the difference between that and 'astrologers'.
• Give an example of how the repetition of words has been used to create pace and atmosphere in the text.
• The word 'terribly' has been used deliberately seven times in one sentence. Explain why you think Ted Hughes chose to do this.

SESSION AIMS

Consider if the readers' attitude towards Hogarth and the Iron Man has changed, and if so why, and identify the underlying messages in the story.

BEFORE THE SESSION

The children should have re-read Chapter 4, identifying effective language use.

READ

- Begin by asking the children to share any language use from the previous chapter that they found to be interesting and effective, explaining the reasons for their selection. Remind them that Ted Hughes is primarily known for his poetry, and was previously Poet Laureate, explaining what this is. Do they think the way he uses language in his story-telling shows that he is a poet?

- Invite the children to suggest what the Iron Man's challenge might involve before reading the final chapter.

During reading

- Ask the children to read the opening paragraph of Chapter 5 independently and in silence. Ask: *How does this show the way the people of the earth feel about the Iron Man? How has this changed from when he first appeared? Why might that be?*

- Ask them also to consider how the Iron Man must feel about the people, as he allows them to take him to pieces. Would they have expected this at the beginning of the story?

- Now ask the children to read the rest of the final chapter in silence. As they read, ask them to think about the character of the Iron Man and their own attitude towards him.

- If your school uses reading journals then the children should be encouraged to make notes as they read and consider each question.

- Move around the group and 'tune in' to hear individuals read aloud. Encourage and praise good expression.

REVISIT AND RESPOND

Use the following discussion points to help the children think about what they have read in more depth.

Note: Since there are only 20 minutes for each session, you are advised to focus on only one or two of the elements that are listed below.

- Talk about the Iron Man's challenge. Ask: *What was your reaction when you read about it? Were you surprised by its nature? Do you think the Iron Man was brave or foolish? Did he expect to win or was he prepared to lose? Did you think he would win? How does his plan show us that he was clever?*

- Why do the children think Ted Hughes made the Iron Man and the space-bat-angel-dragon face each other more than once? What effect would it have had on the story if the space-bat-angel-dragon had given in after the first challenge?

- Encourage the children to consider what evidence there is to tell us that the Iron Man wasn't as fearless as we might have thought earlier in the story. (The paragraph beginning 'At this point, the Iron Man was terribly afraid…' and other phrases, such as 'He could hardly speak after his ordeal…' are clues.)

- Ask the children to recall how Hogarth has been portrayed during the story. Are we told about any friends? How is he similar to the Iron Man? Why are they portrayed as lone figures who are different to the farmers and other people?

- Discuss the message of the story and how it relates to real life. What stories have they seen/heard on the news that could be related to events in the story?

- Invite the children to analyse their feelings towards Hogarth and the Iron Man over the course of the story.

Ask the children, whenever appropriate, to revisit the text to exemplify/support their answers.

Encourage the children to read aloud to the group when referring back to the text – praise clear, confident and expressive reading.

ASSESSMENT OPPORTUNITIES

The following bank of question prompts provides a quick and easy means of monitoring the children's comprehension skills and understanding of the text. The children's answers to a question must be supported by evidence from the text.

Understanding

- How was the Iron Man taken to Australia?
- What had the Iron Man ordered?
- What test did the Iron Man challenge the space-bat-angel-dragon to?
- What happened to the Iron Man the first time he lay on the fiery bed?
- What colours did the Iron Man's body become as he cooled down?
- Why did the space-bat-angel-dragon come to the earth?
- What happened when the space-bat-angel-dragon landed back on earth?
- What effect did the fires of the sun have on the space-bat-angel-dragon the first time he went?
- What did the Iron Man know could happen to him if the flames became even more fierce?
- What did the Iron Man do to make the space-bat-angel-dragon think he was not afraid?
- How did the Iron Man get the space-bat-angel-dragon to leave the earth?
- What presents were sent to the Iron Man?
- Why did the Iron Man not speak to the space-bat-angel-dragon after surviving the fiery bed for the second time? What did he do instead?
- What was the reaction of the space-bat-angel-dragon when he knew the Iron Man was prepared for a 'Round three'?
- What did the space-bat-angel-dragon say was the effect of the music of the spheres?
- What made the space-bat-angel-dragon get 'greedy and cruel ideas'?
- What effect did the space-bat-angel-dragon's singing have on the people of the earth?

Inferences

- Why do you think the world went along with the Iron Man's plan?
- Why do you think the space-bat-angel-dragon was 'astounded' by the Iron Man's challenge?
- The space-bat-angel-dragon 'could flatten the Iron Man with one eyelash'. Why do you think he didn't?
- Why do you think the Iron Man smiled when the flames made him so hot?
- What do you think everyone watching the challenge thought? What did they expect to happen?
- Why do you think the space-bat-angel-dragon continued with the Iron Man's challenge?
- Do you think the Iron Man would have survived a 'Round three'?

Main ideas

- Why were the people frightened of the Iron Man at the beginning of the story? Was this fair? How had their attitude towards him changed at the end, and why was this?
- Who had changed during the story – the Iron Man or the people? Explain your answer.

Themes and conventions

- What message is the author trying to deliver by using Hogarth and the Iron Man to change the ways of the space-bat-angel-dragon?

SESSION 1: MEET GREG

Familiarise with the key characters, and the form and style of the book.

BEFORE THE SESSION

The children should have read the first entry (Tuesday) in Greg's journal independently prior to the session.

READ

- Ask the children about the journal style of the book. Invite the group to comment on the following points:
  - The handwriting-style font and use of lined paper.
  - The inclusion of cartoons and speech bubbles.
- Ask the children: *What does the first entry tell you about the character of Greg?* Focusing on the setting, ask: *What clues are there to tell you in which country the story is set?* (For example, words such as 'jerk', 'Mom', 'middle school', 'grade levels', 'first grade', 'elementary school' all point to it being set in the USA.)
- Invite a volunteer to read Wednesday's entry, asking the group to listen out for any further clues to the American setting. Briefly discuss these before asking the children to read to the end of the following Tuesday's entry independently, ending with 'take a shower'.

During reading
- As they read, ask the children to focus on the new main characters – Rodrick, Manny, Rowley, Mom and Dad – and how Greg seems to feel about them, making notes if they wish.
- Ask them to take note of how the cartoons work within the story, often adding extra information.
- Ask them to consider what they are learning about Greg. What sort of boy is he? How would they describe his character?
- If your school uses reading journals then the children should be encouraged to make notes as they read and consider each question.

- Move around the group and 'tune in' to hear individuals read aloud. Encourage and praise good expression.

REVISIT AND RESPOND

Use the following discussion points to help the children think about what they have read in more depth.

Note: Since there are only 20 minutes for each session, you are advised to focus on only one or two of the elements that are listed below.

- Consider the American setting. Would the story work if it was set in another country? Does the use of American English add to the story or complicate it? As a group, list any examples of Americanisms, discussing possible meanings of any unfamiliar words or expressions.
- Focus on the images. Would the story be as effective without the use of cartoons?
- How would it affect the story if it had not been written as a journal, but told as a conventional third-person narrative?
- Talk about Greg. Ask: *What have we learned about him so far?* Remind the children that we only know what Greg chooses to tell us, so we have to use this information and the way he tells it to work out what he is like – we don't hear directly about him from others.
- Compare and contrast the key supporting characters: Rodrick, Manny, Rowley, Mom and Dad. As a group, make a list of words to describe each of them, referring to Greg's journal entries to support suggestions. Can the children suggest how each character might feel about Greg?
- Look together at the Wednesday entry about the 'Cheese Touch'. What are their thoughts about this? Why would people believe in this superstition?
- From what he tells us, Greg doesn't seem to like Rowley much, even though he calls him his 'best friend'. Can the children suggest why he remains friendly with him?
- What might Greg's teachers say about Greg?

Ask the children, whenever appropriate, to revisit the text to exemplify/support their answers.

Encourage the children to read aloud to the group when referring back to the text – praise clear, confident and expressive reading.

Before the next session
Ask the children to read to the end of the September entry, focusing on Rodrick's band, Greg and the CD, the differences between Mom's and Dad's ways of dealing with Greg's bad behaviour and the posters for student governor elections.

ASSESSMENT OPPORTUNITIES
The following bank of question prompts provides a quick and easy means of monitoring the children's comprehension skills and understanding of the text. The children's answers to a question must be supported by evidence from the text.

Understanding
- At what time of year does Greg's journal begin?
- From whose point of view is Greg's story told?
- Why does Greg begin his journal?
- In which country is the story set?
- Who are the members of Greg's family?
- Why did Greg want to be in the 'Easy' reading group at school?
- Why does Manny call Greg 'Bubby' and how does Greg feel about it?

Inferences
- What kind of person does Greg seem to be? Explain your opinion.
- How does Greg feel about his baby brother, Manny? How do you know?
- Do Greg's Mom and Dad seem happy with the way he behaves? Give examples from the story to support your answer.
- Greg tells us that he likes girls. What might the girls think of him? Why?
- What similarities are there between the way Rodrick behaves towards Greg, and the way Greg behaves towards Manny?

Predicting
- What sort of year do you think Greg will have at school, and why?
- Do you think Greg's friendship with Rowley will last?

Main ideas
- Describe Greg's attitude to school.

Language, structure and presentation
- What has the author used to tell the story, alongside the written text?
- How do the cartoons help to tell the story?
- Is the story told in the first or the third person?
- What American-English words do you remember from this section, and what do they mean?
- What is unusual about the font and the paper it is written on? Why has the author chosen this form of presentation?
- Why might the author have chosen to begin Greg's journal at the start of the school year?

Themes and conventions
- We are used to books being divided into chapters. Why are there no chapter divisions in this book?
- What do you notice about the writing in the speech bubbles?

▼ SESSION 2: HALLOWEEN

SESSION AIMS

Learn more about the main character, including his relationship with other key characters.

BEFORE THE SESSION

The children should have read to the end of September's entry.

READ

- As a group, invite the children to recall the events from the entries for September that they have read since the previous session. Ask: *How do you think Rodrick felt when he discovered that Greg had taken and listened to his CD?* Ask: *What differences are there in how Greg's Mom and Dad deal with their son's bad behaviour?* For example, Dad gets angry quickly, then calms down and the incident is over with, whereas Mom thinks about things for a while before deciding what Greg's punishment should be. Ask: *Was the teacher right to take down Greg's posters?*

- Ask the children to scan the section in Wednesday's entry about Rodrick's band, beginning 'Rodrick's band is REALLY awful,' up to 'She's the one who bought Rodrick his first drum set'. From what we have read of Mom so far, this does not seem typical of her. What are the children's views on her encouraging Rodrick's music-making?

- Look together at the cartoon in Friday's entry, where Dad is saying 'LET'S YOU AND ME HAVE A TALK, FRIEND.' Ask: *Why is the word 'friend' in bigger letters?*

During reading

- Invite a volunteer to read the first three paragraphs of the opening entry for October. Ask: *How does the author make this funny? What do you think of Dad's actions?*

- Ask the children to read on to the end of the Saturday entry, about Greg and Rowley's haunted house. Ask them to consider what problems they can see in the boys' plan.

- If your school uses reading journals then the children should be encouraged to make notes as they read and consider each question.

- Move around the group and 'tune in' to hear individuals read aloud. Encourage and praise good expression.

REVISIT AND RESPOND

Use the following discussion points to help the children think about what they have read in more depth.

Note: Since there are only 20 minutes for each session, you are advised to focus on only one or two of the elements that are listed below.

- Even though they expected their visit to the Crossland haunted house to be scary, Greg and Rowley were keen to go. Why might this have been such an attraction for them?

- What more have the children learned about Greg from this section? What words would they use to describe him?

- Ask the children to look at the boys' plan for their haunted house. Is the plan easy to follow, for example by using the arrows? Did Greg and Rowley have good ideas? Are there any ways they might have made some of their ideas actually work?

- Look together at the boys' poster for their haunted house. Is it set out well? Does it include everything that is needed for an effective poster? Can the children see any problems with what is included?

- Although Greg's Mom took the boys to visit the Crossland haunted house, she wouldn't allow Greg to make his own in their house. What could be her reason(s) for this?

- Why do you think Rowley didn't tell his parents about their haunted house plans? What do you think Rowley's father might say to Greg's Mom about it?

Ask the children, whenever appropriate, to revisit the text to exemplify/support their answers.

Encourage the children to read aloud to the group when referring back to the text – praise clear, confident and expressive reading.

Before the next session

The children should read to the end of the October entry, making notes about the events. Ask them to look out for the effects Mom has on Greg's trick-or-treating, and to list the things that go wrong for the boys.

ASSESSMENT OPPORTUNITIES

The following bank of question prompts provides a quick and easy means of monitoring the children's comprehension skills and understanding of the text. The children's answers to a question must be supported by evidence from the text.

Understanding

- What changes did Greg and Rowley make from their original haunted house plan and poster?
- How do we know that Greg's father enjoyed Halloween?
- Why did Greg begin to have second thoughts about going in to the Crossland haunted house?
- How did Greg's Mom react to the person with a chainsaw at the Crossland haunted house?
- What gave Greg the idea to make a haunted house of his own?
- What was holding up the flow of children visiting Greg and Rowley's haunted house?

Inferences

- Judging by his behaviour at Halloween, what do you think Greg's Dad would have been like as a child?
- What reasons could there be for the Crossland haunted house being a success, while Greg's and Rowley's was a failure?
- Why do you think Greg's Mom was in a hurry to get through the Crossland haunted house?
- How much do you think Rowley had a say in the haunted house being built in his basement?

Predicting

- What do you think will happen to Greg and Rowley now that Rowley's father has discovered what they did?

Main ideas

- Considering the events in the entries for September and October so far, what do you notice about Greg's various plans? He is enthusiastic and full of ideas, but is he successful?

Language, structure and presentation

- What would be the British-English equivalents to the following American-English words:
  - candy
  - trash can
  - five bucks a pop?
- Greg tried to show Rowley's father that they were 'running a legitimate operation'. What does this mean?
- Why might the author have told us about Greg and Rowley's visit to the Crossland haunted house before we read about them making their own?

▼ SESSION 3: WRESTLING

SESSION AIMS

Consider different characters' reactions and responses to the same stimulus.

BEFORE THE SESSION

The children should have read to the end of the October entries, making notes on events.

READ

- Invite the children to share the notes they made from the October entries, about Greg and Rowley's trick-or-treating. In what ways did they find that Greg's Mom influenced the events of the night? For example, by providing Greg's costume, insisting he take Manny and that Dad accompany them, and then telling Greg and Rowley they must come home when they are avoiding the teenagers at Gramma's house.
- Ask them to share their lists of the things that went wrong for the boys while they were trick-or-treating. Ask: *Could any of these things have been avoided?*
- The older boys are allowed to be out without an adult at night. What are the children's reactions to this? Ask: *What does this show you about the parents' trust in the boys and in the neighbourhood?*
- Invite the children to share what they thought were the funniest parts of the night's events.
- What did they think about Dad soaking the boys when they got home?
- Then ask the children to read Wednesday's, Thursday's and Tuesday's entries for November.

During reading

- As they read, ask them to focus on what more they are learning about Greg.
- Invite the children to take particular note of how the cartoons work with the written text in this section.
- If your school uses reading journals then the children should be encouraged to make notes as they read and consider each question.
- Move around the group and 'tune in' to hear

individuals read aloud. Encourage and praise good expression.

- When the children have read this section, ask them to consider Greg's reactions to learning about the wrestling unit. Have a brief discussion about the character of Greg, now that we have learned more about him. Ask: *Does he show initiative? Is he foolish? Is he an enthusiast? Does he annoy people? Does he realise that his plans always seem to go wrong?*

REVISIT AND RESPOND

Use the following discussion points to help the children think about what they have read in more depth.

Note: Since there are only 20 minutes for each session, you are advised to focus on only one or two of the elements that are listed below.

- What questions would the children want to ask Greg's teacher, Mom and Dad about the wrestling and Greg's body-building plans?
- Invite the children to find ways in which Greg annoys other people in this section. Do they think he is aware of how others react to him? Why, or why not?
- Once again, we see Greg's plans proving to be unsuccessful. Ask the children for examples of this, inviting them to explain why the plans have gone wrong.
- How did Greg's Mom and Dad respond differently to his body-building plan? Can the children explain why this might be?

Ask the children, whenever appropriate, to revisit the text to exemplify/support their answers.

Encourage the children to read aloud to the group when referring back to the text – praise clear, confident and expressive reading.

Before the next session

The children should read to the end of the entries for November. Ask them to think about how Greg behaves at school, with Rowley and with his parents. When is he well behaved?

ASSESSMENT OPPORTUNITIES

The following bank of question prompts provides a quick and easy means of monitoring the children's comprehension skills and understanding of the text. The children's answers to a question must be supported by evidence from the text.

Understanding
- The November entry opens with the aftermath of Halloween at Gramma's house. What is the children's opinion of Greg's response to this?
- Do you agree with Greg's first thoughts about the school having a wrestling unit?
- When he found out what the wrestling involved, why was Greg disappointed?
- What did Greg do to try to avoid wrestling Fregley?

Inferences
- Does the wrestling unit include the girls in the school?
- How do we know who Greg practised his wrestling holds on? Who was it?

Predicting
- At the end of Tuesday's entry, Greg says that he will have to take matters into his own hands about his body-building plan. What do you think he might do?
- Do you think Greg will succeed in his body building? Do you think he will be successful in the wrestling? Why, or why not?

Main ideas
- Compare what you think the school, Greg, Rowley and Greg's parents think about the idea of a wrestling unit.

Language, structure and presentation
- Make a list of words used in this section that are specifically related to wrestling (for example, 'pile drivers', 'ring', 'holds', 'half nelson', 'reversal', 'takedown', 'fireman's carry'). Do you know what they all mean? Does it affect your understanding if you don't know their exact meaning?
- Greg talks about teams of 'shirts' and 'skins'. How does the accompanying cartoon help us to understand what this means?

Themes and conventions
- Once again, we see examples of how things never seem to go right for Greg – a key theme of the book. Ask the children to find examples in this section of the text, and recall previous incidents where things have gone wrong for him. Can they explain why this might be?
- Even though things always seem to go wrong for Greg, the author has told his story in a humorous way. Can the children suggest why this might be? Is he using humour to get across the message that Greg's way is not the right way to behave? Or is he just having fun, writing a funny book?

SESSION AIMS

Observe how the actions of one character can impact upon the story.

BEFORE THE SESSION

The children should have read to the end of the entries for November, focusing on Greg's behaviour.

READ

- Begin the session by asking the children to recap on their reading since the previous session, which started when Greg was undertaking his own body-building programme.
- Ask the children what home-made equipment Greg used. What are their views on how he used Rowley as his training partner? What does this show us about Greg, and about Rowley?
- The rest of the November section is about Greg trying out for the school musical. Talk together about how Greg behaves when his Mom tells him she wants him to take part. Does Greg do what he is told? It's clear he doesn't want to audition, but here we see him doing what his mother tells him.
- Ask the children why Greg decides he wants to be a tree in the school production, and why he is disappointed in his costume.
- Ask the children to comment on how Greg behaves with Rowley, at school and with his parents.
- Now invite the children to read December's entries, up to the end of Wednesday. This section focuses on the school musical performance.

During reading

- Ask them to make a note of all the things that go wrong during the performance.
- Ask them to think of any questions that arise as they read.
- If your school uses reading journals then the children should be encouraged to make notes as they read and consider each question.

- Move around the group and 'tune in' to hear individuals read aloud. Encourage and praise good expression.
- When the children have finished reading, invite them to share their observations of what went wrong during the performance. Ask: *Why did these things happen? Was anyone to blame?* Invite them to share some of the questions they have formulated, inviting others in the group to answer them.

REVISIT AND RESPOND

Use the following discussion points to help the children think about what they have read in more depth.

Note: Since there are only 20 minutes for each session, you are advised to focus on only one or two of the elements that are listed below.

- Mrs Norton is in charge of the play. Discuss what her feelings were likely to be after the performance.
- What do the children think the audience's reaction would have been to the play? Would they have realised that things had gone wrong?
- How would Patty Farrell feel after the performance?
- Greg tells us that he wanted to get his own back at Patty Farrell for making the geography test harder for him. Do the children think he succeeded in this? Was what he did fair?
- Imagine the conversation that Greg's parents would have when they got home after the performance. Ask: *What do you think they might say to Greg and to each other? Would Mom and Dad feel the same way about it?*
- Ask the children to choose the part of this section that they found the funniest, giving reasons for their choice.
- Talk about the part played by the cartoons in telling the story. Would it be as successful without them?

Ask the children, whenever appropriate, to revisit the text to exemplify/support their answers.

Encourage the children to read aloud to the group when referring back to the text – praise clear, confident and expressive reading.

Before the next session

Ask the children to read to the end of the entries for December, considering the kind of Christmas that Greg has and how he would feel about it.

ASSESSMENT OPPORTUNITIES

The following bank of question prompts provides a quick and easy means of monitoring the children's comprehension skills and understanding of the text. The children's answers to a question must be supported by evidence from the text.

Understanding

- Why did Greg decide he wanted to be a tree in the school musical?
- In what way does Mrs Norton make it difficult for the children to learn their lines for the school play?
- What happened to hold up the start of the performance?
- Why and how were the trees' costumes changed?
- What did Greg do to contribute towards things going wrong in the performance?
- What did Greg do to try to make everyone think that someone else had the nickname 'Bubby'?
- Why did the trees stop singing?
- Why did Greg's Mom throw the flowers away after the performance?

Inferences

- Why would the audience not be convinced about the character of Dorothy's dog Toto?
- How would Greg feel when he saw his brother Rodrick in the audience?
- How do we know that Greg's Mom was annoyed with him?
- How do we know that Greg enjoyed the performance?

Predicting

- What do you think would happen the next day at school? What would the teachers say, and what would the children's reactions be? What would Patty Farrell have to say?

Main ideas

- This incident shows us how the actions of one or two characters can impact upon the story, taking it forward and giving it pace. It also tells us more about the nature of the characters involved. Ask the children how the story might have been different here, if the author had chosen for the performance to go well. Also, invite the children to look back to the events around the geography test, asking them how this small incident had a direct effect upon what happened during the performance.

Language, structure and presentation

- Ask the children to note vocabulary linked to a performance (for example, 'lines', 'stage', 'audience', 'performance', 'curtains', 'play', 'stage fright').

▼ SESSION 5: THE BIG WHEEL AND THE ROBOT

SESSION AIMS

Develop further understanding of the character of Greg through his actions and attitudes.

BEFORE THE SESSION

The children should have read the remainder of the entries for December, where Greg tells us about the events of Christmas and New Year.

READ

- Ask the children to recap Greg's Christmas from their reading prior to the session. Did he have a good time?
- Do they think Greg was being genuinely kind to Manny when he advised him to circle just a few items in the catalogue? Manny ignored him and received everything he had circled. How do they think Greg felt?
- What happened when Greg asked Uncle Charlie for the Barbie Dream House?
- What more do we learn about Rodrick in this section? How might his behaviour have influenced Greg as he was growing up? Might Greg's behaviour have the same effect upon Manny? How does the incident with the spider suggest that Manny is learning from Greg?
- Dad had kept his promise to give Greg weight-training equipment for Christmas, but Greg is now not interested in it any more. How would Dad feel when he realised that Greg was not thrilled with his well-meaning present?
- Ask the children to read the entries for January, to the end of the second Tuesday, ending with 'how it all got started'.

During reading
- As they read, ask them to consider what more can be learned about Greg from this section.
- They may find some references to the American education system that are unfamiliar. Ask them to make a note of any words or phrases they don't know, for later clarification.
- If your school uses reading journals then the children should be encouraged to make notes as they read and consider each question.
- Move around the group and 'tune in' to hear individuals read aloud. Encourage and praise good expression.

REVISIT AND RESPOND

Use the following discussion points to help the children think about what they have read in more depth.

Note: Since there are only 20 minutes for each session, you are advised to focus on only one or two of the elements that are listed below.

- Why do you think Rowley does what Greg tells him? Why does he remain Greg's friend after the way he is treated? Is this the way to treat a friend?
- Was Greg's thank-you letter idea on the computer a good one? What could he have done to make it work?
- How do we know that Greg wasn't sympathetic when Rowley broke his hand?
- What do you think Rowley's and Greg's parents would have said when they learned about Rowley's accident with the Big Wheel?
- Why do you think the school allows children to work without a teacher? Why does everyone in the group get the same grade?
- Greg gets up first to suggest ideas for the robot plans. What does this tell us about him? He seems confident and enthusiastic, and willing to share his ideas, but is he just showing off and wanting his own way?
- Greg suggests by his comments that the girls have silly ideas for the robot, but the boys are the real workers. What does this tell us about his attitude towards girls? How does this sit alongside his previous comments that he likes girls and wants to impress them?
- Ask the children to consider the honesty with which Greg relates the things that happen to him. He seems not to worry that he is showing himself

in a poor light, including in the cartoons he draws. We know that he does see the journal as being something others might read in the future, because he tells us in his first entry that it will be useful when he becomes 'rich and famous'.

Ask the children, whenever appropriate, to revisit the text to exemplify/support their answers.

Encourage the children to read aloud to the group when referring back to the text – praise clear, confident and expressive reading.

Before the next session

Ask the children to read up to the end of the entries for April. Invite the children to note the positive and negative elements of each of the three incidents in this section – Greg volunteering for Safety Patrol and its ultimate consequences, Greg and Rowley building a snowman and Greg applying for the job of cartoonist on the school paper.

ASSESSMENT OPPORTUNITIES

The following bank of question prompts provides a quick and easy means of monitoring the children's comprehension skills and understanding of the text. The children's answers to a question must be supported by evidence from the text.

Understanding

- What game did Greg invent for using the Big Wheel that Rowley gave him for Christmas?

- How was Rowley involved in the game?

- What did Greg do to get attention after Rowley broke his hand?

- Why did the boys like having Ricky Fisher in their group? How did this lead to the boys' Independent Study being cancelled?

- Why did Greg's computer-generated thank-you letters not work every time?

- Why did Greg's bandaged arm idea not work for him in the way that Rowley's cast did?

- When the children learned that they weren't going to actually build a robot, but just make plans for one, how do you think they would feel?

Inferences

- How do we know that Greg does what his Mom tells him in this section?

- How might Rowley feel at always having to be the one to use the Big Wheel and have a ball thrown at him?

- How do we know that Greg is jealous of the attention Rowley gets after he broke his hand?

Predicting

- The Independent Study class was an experiment at Greg's school. Do you think they will offer this class again? Why, or why not?

Main ideas

- In this section we see more of the way in which Greg treats his best friend Rowley, through the Big Wheel game and his attitude afterwards. What are the children's opinions of Greg now? Would they like to have him as a friend? Why, or why not?

▼ SESSION 6: THE END OF A FRIENDSHIP

SESSION AIMS

Summarise the main character of the book.

BEFORE THE SESSION

The children should have read up to the end of April's entries, making notes about the three incidents.

READ

- Begin by asking the children to share their notes about the negative and positive aspects of the three incidents they have recently read, from January, February, March and April's entries. Briefly discuss their observations.
  - Was it fair when Dad smashed Greg's and Rowley's giant snowball? Why, or why not? Why did he do it?
  - Did Greg have any justification for thinking he would get the job of cartoonist on the school paper? Give your reasons.
  - What do the children think of Greg's, Rowley's and the other children's comic strips?
  - What do they think about Mr Ira changing Greg's comic strip?
- Rowley finally seems to have had enough of the way Greg treats him, when he is blamed for the worm incident with the kindergarteners. Again, Greg doesn't seem to realise that his behaviour is unacceptable. Discuss Greg's behaviour.
- Can the children suggest why this time Rowley decides to end his friendship with Greg, and why Greg wants Rowley to be his friend again?
- Do the children think that losing Rowley's friendship might make Greg realise that he needs to behave differently in future?
- We know from previous entries that Greg has a low opinion of Fregley, but he chooses him to be his new friend when Rowley breaks up with him. Could it be because he doesn't have any other choice? Can they think of any other children he has mentioned

as being his friends? What reasons can they suggest for Greg having so few friends?

- What do they think about Greg's idea for getting mentioned in the class yearbook?

Ask the children to read to the end of the book.

During reading

- Invite them to consider Greg's reactions to what happens.
- Ask them to look out for events from much earlier in the book that are now seen to have an impact on the end of the story.
- If your school uses reading journals then the children should be encouraged to make notes as they read and consider each question.
- Move around the group and 'tune in' to hear individuals read aloud. Encourage and praise good expression.
- Briefly discuss what the children have noticed.

REVISIT AND RESPOND

Use the following discussion points to help the children think about what they have read in more depth.

Note: Since there are only 20 minutes for each session, you are advised to focus on only one or two of the elements that are listed below.

- What would Greg's classmates have thought when his Mom turned up as their substitute teacher?
- Do the children think Greg would behave differently in school when his Mom was his teacher? Would the other teachers tell her what he is normally like in school?
- Greg is surprised and annoyed when Rowley's comic strip is a success. Is Rowley better off without Greg as his friend?
- Why was Greg reluctant to fight Rowley?
- Can the children work out what the teenagers made Rowley do with the cheese?
- In what ways can we see that Greg might have changed a little (for example, he chose not to mention to Rowley that he could have used some of his karate moves, and he pretended that he had

moved the cheese instead of telling everyone that Rowley had been made to eat it).

- We have now read Greg's journal for the full school year. Overall, what is the children's opinion of Greg? Has it changed in any way as they have read the book?

- What do they think Greg's teachers would say about him at the end of the year? What might be in his school report?

- Do they think Greg and Rowley will remain friends? If so, would their friendship be any different in future, because of what happened at the end of the book?

- What words would they use to describe Greg?

- What would they say to recommend the book to other readers?

Ask the children, whenever appropriate, to revisit the text to exemplify/support their answers.

Encourage the children to read aloud to the group when referring back to the text – praise clear, confident and expressive reading.

ASSESSMENT OPPORTUNITIES

The following bank of question prompts provides a quick and easy means of monitoring the children's comprehension skills and understanding of the text. The children's answers to a question must be supported by evidence from the text.

Understanding

- Why was Greg looking forward to having a substitute teacher?

- Why had Greg quit his job as school cartoonist?

- What was the catchphrase of Rowley's comic strip?

- How did Greg and Rowley get involved in a fight?

- Why did the teenagers turn up looking for Greg and Rowley?

Inferences

- How did Greg feel when he discovered that Rowley was the new school cartoonist?

- Why do you think Greg told everyone that he had moved the cheese?

Predicting

- How do you think Greg will behave towards Rowley in the future? Why?

- How do you think Rowley will behave in his renewed friendship with Greg?

Main ideas

- In what two ways does Greg behave unexpectedly towards Rowley after the teenagers come to get them?

- How would you describe the character of Greg?

- Is Greg a good role model? Why, or why not?

Language, structure and presentation

- Overall, how would you say the mixture of written text and cartoons works in the book?

Themes and conventions

- In what ways can the book be said to be about friendship?

- Give some examples to show that one theme of the book is behaviour towards others.

SESSION 1: MEETING DANNY AND HIS DAD

SESSION AIMS

Checking that a text makes sense to them and discussing how an author introduces a story and its main characters.

BEFORE THE SESSION

The children should have read Chapters 1 and 2 independently prior to the session.

READ

- Ask the children to remind themselves of what happens in Chapters 1 and 2, while thinking about the following points:
  - What sort of boy is Danny?
  - What kind of life does he live?
  - What is Danny's relationship with his father like?
- After they have done this, ask them to read Chapter 3 independently, keeping the above questions in mind.

REVISIT AND RESPOND

Use the following discussion points to help the children think about what they have read in more depth.

Note: Since there are only 20 minutes for each session, you are advised to focus on only one or two of the elements that are listed below.

- Read the description, in Chapter 1, of the gypsy caravan where Danny lives and discuss whether Danny is happy to live there or not. Invite the children to identify parts from the text that show how he feels about his home. Ask: *Would you like to live in a caravan like that? Would you like to live in just one room with your family, with an outside toilet?* The children could make a list of the pros and cons of living in their house or Danny's caravan, and you could take a vote at the end to see where people would rather live.

- At the beginning of Chapter 2, Danny describes how his father smiles more with his eyes than with his mouth, and says that mouth-smiles can be faked. Ask the children what he means by this and whether they agree with him. Does either way look better – or worse? They could attempt to smile just with their mouths, just with their eyes and then both, then ask a partner which looks better.

- Danny says that his father was not an educated man and that he doubts 'if he had read twenty books in his life'. Ask the children if having a good education, or being well read, is important? Does this matter in life? Does it mean that someone is a better person if they have read a lot of books or had a good education? In pairs, ask the children to make a list of the advantages and disadvantages of having a good education and reading many books, and then share the results with the rest of the class.

- Most of Chapter 2 is taken up by Danny's father telling the story of 'The Big Friendly Giant'. Explain to the children that Roald Dahl wrote this chapter before then expanding it into a full-length novel of its own. Ask: *Have you read The BFG?* If they have, invite opinions on how this chapter compares to the finished novel. How is the story the same or different? If some children haven't read the novel, ask them if they would like to, based on what they have read in Chapter 2.

- Danny's father makes a lot of things for his son. Invite the children to look back through Chapter 3 and make a note of the various toys and other objects that he makes. Ask them: *Why does Danny's father make toys for his son, rather than buy them? Which would you rather have – a home-made toy or something from a shop?* You could encourage the children to give examples of presents that friends or family have made them, and what they felt like when they received them. Finally, ask: *Do you think the presents would be the same if Danny's mother had lived?*

Ask the children, whenever appropriate, to revisit the text to exemplify/support their answers.

Encourage the children to read aloud to the group when referring back to the text – praise clear, confident and expressive reading.

Before the next session
Ask the children to read Chapters 4 and 5.

ASSESSMENT OPPORTUNITIES

The following bank of question prompts provides a quick and easy means of monitoring the children's comprehension skills and understanding of the text. The children's answers to a question must be supported by evidence from the text.

Understanding
- How old was Danny when his mother died?
- Where do Danny and his father live?
- Where does Danny's father work? What does he do?
- How do they keep their caravan warm and light?
- What two things did Danny and his father make and fly?

Inferences
- How do Danny and his father feel about Danny's mother's death?
- Are Danny and his father close?
- Did Danny's father really see 'The Big Friendly Giant'?
- How do you think Danny felt about starting school later than other children?
- Do you think Danny will still want to be a mechanic when he grows up?

Predicting
- Will Danny and his father get in trouble for Danny not starting school when he was five years old?
- Will Danny and his father carry on being happy together?
- What might happen to Danny that could be 'exciting' but not 'fun'?

Main ideas
- Look at how Danny and his father live, and discuss whether people can be happy in life with very few material goods. What is more important – a loving home or a home that is big and has electricity and heating?

Language, structure and presentation
- What effect does it have on the reader to have 'The BFG' as a bedtime story in Chapter 2?
- The author uses ellipses (…) a lot when Danny's father is speaking (such as at the start of Chapter 3). Why does he do this? What effect does this have on the text? What do the ellipses show about how he is speaking?

SESSION 2: POACHER'S BOTTOM

Participate in discussions and take turns and listen to what others say.

BEFORE THE SESSION

The children should have read Chapters 4 and 5 independently before the session.

READ

- Ask the children to remind themselves of what happens in Chapters 4 and 5, while thinking about the following points:
  - Is poaching an art or stealing, or both?
  - Are there any better or worse ways to kill pheasants? (For example, is poaching better than making them fat and tame, and then killing them?)
- Ask them to read Chapters 6 and 7 independently.

During reading

- Bear in mind how Mr Hazell is described and the way he behaves.
- If your school uses reading journals then the children should be encouraged to make notes as they read and consider each question.
- Move around the group and 'tune in' to hear individuals read aloud. Encourage and praise good expression.

REVISIT AND RESPOND

Use the following discussion points to help the children think about what they have read in more depth.

Note: Since there are only 20 minutes for each session, you are advised to focus on only one or two of the elements that are listed below.

- Revisit the explanation that Danny's father gives about why he poaches and why his father, in turn, used to do it (for food). Ask them why Danny's father still does it (for excitement) and if this is as good a reason. Then, look at the explanation of what Mr Hazell does with his pheasants (he buys them young, fattens them up and then shoots them when they are tame). Ask: *Is what Mr Hazell does worse than poaching?* Invite them to debate when killing animals is acceptable (if it is) and when it isn't.

- Danny's father leaves him at night time to go out poaching. Ask: *Is it responsible or sensible to leave Danny on his own? Would this be allowed nowadays?* Then, ask them to consider if Danny would be scared to be left alone, even if he knew where his father was. Would they be afraid to be left alone? What would they have done if they were Danny and had discovered their father was missing – would they have gone out to look for him? Was this brave or foolish?

- Consider how Mr Hazell is portrayed in the book. Roald Dahl makes no secret of the fact that he is the 'bad guy', but how does he show this through his descriptions, either through Danny's father's words or Danny's? Ask the the children: *Why is Mr Hazell a 'roaring snob'? Why is he so desperate to 'get in with what he believed were the right kind of people'? Is there a 'right kind'?* Ask them if any particular type of people are better than another. Would they do things to make themselves popular with people they admired? Have they ever done this and, if so, did it work? Did they feel they were being themselves when they did it?

- Look at the concept of revenge, relating it to what happened to Danny and his father after they refused to serve Mr Hazell at their filling station. Why did so many inspectors come to visit Danny and his father and what were they trying to do? Why would Mr Hazell be so furious with them – was it only because they refused to serve him? Ask: *How did Danny's father come to have such a tiny piece of land on the Hazell estate? Wouldn't he want to move away from it if he could, since he doesn't like him?*

- Look at the pages in Chapter 7 where Danny describes getting the Baby Austin ready to drive, through to his journey on the road. Ask: *How does the author create tension and suspense in these pages?* They should hopefully recognise the use of shorter, sharper sentences, the repetition of certain words (such as 'bigger and bigger', 'nearer and nearer') and the use of violent verbs ('yanked', 'swerved violently', 'roared'). Next, ask the children to work in pairs, describing the scene in their own words. They should either aim for the same effect of suspense or they could create more of a sinister, slow atmosphere.

Ask the children, whenever appropriate, to revisit the text to exemplify/support their answers.

Encourage the children to read aloud to the group when referring back to the text – praise clear, confident and expressive reading.

Before the next session
Ask the children to read Chapters 8 and 9.

ASSESSMENT OPPORTUNITIES
The following bank of question prompts provides a quick and easy means of monitoring the children's comprehension skills and understanding of the text. The children's answers to a question must be supported by evidence from the text.

Understanding
- What is a 'quirk'?
- What is poaching?
- What are pheasants crazy about?
- How many methods did Danny's father suggest to catch pheasants? Can you list them?
- What is twilight?
- Name the car that Danny drives to rescue his father.

Inferences
- Why was Danny so upset when his Dad was missing? What might he have thought had happened to him?
- What would the police have said about a boy driving a car?
- Why is Mr Hazell a 'snob'?

Predicting
- Will Danny find his father?
- Will the owner of the Baby Austin realise his car was used?

Language, structure and presentation
- What does the expression 'to have something hidden up your sleeve' mean?
- What does the metaphor 'the silence was deadly' mean?
- What does 'half-baked' mean?
- How can a voice be 'dangerously soft'?
- On the second page of Chapter 7 there are several sentences and phrases that are written in italics. Why did the author do this?

Themes and conventions
- Look at the different reasons why Danny's father and grandfather poached pheasants and consider whether stealing is ever acceptable. Is it always a crime?

▼ SESSION 3: LEGAL OR ILLEGAL?

SESSION AIMS

Identify how language, structure and presentation contribute to meaning.

BEFORE THE SESSION

The children should have read Chapters 8 and 9 independently before the session.

READ

- Ask the children to remind themselves of what happens in Chapters 8 and 9, while thinking about the following questions:
  - Is Danny brave to rescue his father?
  - Does his father deserve to be captured for breaking the law?
  - Is Doc Spencer's reaction to Mr Hazell and the poachers what you expected?
- Invite them to then read Chapters 10 and 11 independently.

During reading

- Ask them to think about whether poaching is better, worse or the same as shooting tame pheasants at a special party.
- Think about Danny and his role in the story in Chapter 11 – is he cleverer than his father? If they think so, why do they think the author wants them to feel this way?
- If your school uses reading journals then the children should be encouraged to make notes as they read and consider each question.
- Move around the group and 'tune in' to hear individuals read aloud. Encourage and praise good expression.

REVISIT AND RESPOND

Use the following discussion points to help the children think about what they have read in more depth.

Note: Since there are only 20 minutes for each session, you are advised to focus on only one or two of the elements that are listed below.

- Consider how furious Doc Spencer is when he hears that Mr Hazell digs deep pits to trap poachers and how the author uses language to show this anger. Invite the children to think about why he is so angry, especially when Danny's father is the person breaking the law. Do the children agree with Doc Spencer or do they think that Mr Hazell is justified in trying to catch people stealing pheasants on his land? Ask: *Who is committing the worst crime – Danny's father or Mr Hazell? Doc Spencer calls himself and Danny's father 'decent folk' – are they? Is what they do 'a little fun' or is it worse?* Ask the children what they think Roald Dahl's view is, from looking at what the characters say.

- Consider why Danny's father gets so angry when he sees Mr Hazell each morning. Ask: *Why doesn't he just ignore him when he drives past? What does this tell you about Danny's father and how he thinks?* Ask the children what words and language his father uses to show his dislike of Mr Hazell and get them to list examples, including how Mr Hazell is described. Finally, ask them if they have ever felt the same way as Danny's father about someone or something.

- Revisit the description of Mr Hazell's annual pheasant shoot. Ask: *Why do all the people come to the shoot if they think Mr Hazell is 'a nasty piece of work'? Why would someone go to something if they didn't like the person running or hosting it? Would you do that?*

- Danny comes up with a plan to help his father get revenge on Mr Hazell. Ask: *Is Danny's plan a good one? Do you think that the author wants us to think that Danny is cleverer than his father because he thought of a plan that would work when his father could not?* Next, ask the children whether they think Danny's father should be encouraging

Danny to take part in something like this. Is Danny's father being responsible in his behaviour, and in his decision to keep Danny off school so he can help prepare the raisins?

- Look at the preparations Danny and his father make for their plan. Ask the children what Roald Dahl thinks about the plan. Is the way he describes it positive or do they think he disapproves? Can they can see any signs of the author's views and how he uses description, conversation and language to build expectation or excitement in this chapter?

Ask the children, whenever appropriate, to revisit the text to exemplify/support their answers.

Encourage the children to read aloud to the group when referring back to the text – praise clear, confident and expressive reading.

Before the next session
Ask the children to read Chapters 12 and 13.

ASSESSMENT OPPORTUNITIES
The following bank of question prompts provides a quick and easy means of monitoring the children's comprehension skills and understanding of the text. The children's answers to a question must be supported by evidence from the text.

Understanding
- How did Doc Spencer catch trout?
- What did Doc Spencer do to Mr Hazell to punish him for kicking the doctor's dog?
- What does Mrs Spencer give to Danny when his father returns from hospital?
- When does the pheasant shooting season start?
- What do Danny and his father call their new method of catching pheasants?

Inferences
- Why, apart from excitement, do Danny's legs shake when he finds his father?
- What would Mr Hazell have done to Danny's father if he had caught him?
- Why does Danny's father shiver in the pit, despite it being a warm night?

- Why is Danny 'flabbergasted' when he hears that Doc Spencer is a poacher?

Predicting
- Will it take a long time for Danny and his father to prepare all the raisins? Will the plan work?
- Will Danny be in trouble for being off school?
- Will Danny and his father get enough pheasants for the plan to work?

Main ideas
- Danny's father is happy for his son to help him plan for what is an illegal act. Do you think that, as a parent, he should act this way?

Language, structure and presentation
- What does Danny mean when he says: 'I cannot possibly describe to you what it felt like'?
- What is a mechanical shovel?
- What does the word 'flabbergasted' mean?
- Why is Danny's method called 'The Sleeping Beauty'?

SESSION 4: SLEEPY PHEASANTS

SESSION AIMS

Ask and answer questions to improve understanding of a text.

BEFORE THE SESSION

The children should have read Chapters 12 and 13 independently before the session.

READ

- Ask the children to remind themselves of what happens in Chapters 12 and 13, while thinking about the following points:
  - What was school like for Danny and how is this different to their experience?
  - Would they prefer to go to Danny's school?
- Then ask them to read Chapters 14 and 15 independently.

During reading
- Think how both Danny and his father feel when they are getting ready to put their plan into action, and when they finally arrive at the wood.
- Consider whether Danny and his father will succeed in their plan. Ask: *Do you want them to?*
- If your school uses reading journals then the children should be encouraged to make notes as they read and consider each question.
- Move around the group and 'tune in' to hear individuals read aloud. Encourage and praise good expression.

REVISIT AND RESPOND

Use the following discussion points to help the children think about what they have read in more depth.

Note: Since there are only 20 minutes for each session, you are advised to focus on only one or two of the elements that are listed below.

- In Chapter 12, on the walk to school, Danny's father shows his large knowledge of nature and the countryside, and Danny wishes that these facts could be placed on the stone above the school. Ask: *What is your favourite fact from those that Danny lists (shown in capitals) in Chapter 12? Did you know any of these facts already?* Then, ask them if they think it is boring to have the same thing written on a sign all the time, before getting them to make a list of what facts, jokes and sayings they would like written on their school sign.

- Ask the children to think about the punishment given out to Danny and his friend Sidney. Explain that, in the past, children were regularly caned if they misbehaved but that this is now illegal. Ask: *Do you think it is acceptable to hit a child at school if they have been naughty?* What other methods of punishment do the children know of that are used in schools today, and do they think these are better than violence?

- In Chapter 13, Danny's father talks about Danny's mother, and Danny says: 'I never knew quite what to say when he talked about my mother'. Ask the children to re-scan this section of the chapter and discuss what Danny means by this. Is he feeling sad? Worried? Uncomfortable? Why does he feel this way? Ask: *What does Danny mean when he says 'I was beginning to realise what an immense sorrow it must have been to him when she died'? Why had he not realised before?* Are the children impressed that Danny's mother also used to go poaching with his father? Do they think Danny feels that way too?

- In Chapter 14, Danny's father likens what they are doing to 'the greatest game of hide-and-seek in the world'. Ask: *Why is Danny's father so excited about what they are doing? Isn't he nervous, like Danny is?* Then, look at what Danny says about his father becoming 'twitchy' as they get closer to the woods. Do the children think he is excited, nervous or scared? Why does he not sing the proper words to songs? What effect do his nerves have on Danny? How do the children behave when they become nervous? Do they sing to themselves? Ask them to share what they feel and what they do.

Ask the children, whenever appropriate, to revisit the text to exemplify/support their answers.

Encourage the children to read aloud to the group when referring back to the text – praise clear, confident and expressive reading.

Before the next session
Ask the children to read Chapters 16 and 17.

ASSESSMENT OPPORTUNITIES

The following bank of question prompts provides a quick and easy means of monitoring the children's comprehension skills and understanding of the text. The children's answers to a question must be supported by evidence from the text.

Understanding
- What is the name of the apples that Danny picks from his garden?
- How many children are there in Danny's school?
- What did Mr Snoddy have in his glass instead of water?
- What did Danny's father put into the raisins before sewing them shut?
- What did Danny's mother think of the poaching?

Inferences
- When Danny's father has trouble sleeping after Danny has been caned at school, is it from excitement at their plans or something else?
- Why does Danny's father want to confront Captain Lancaster?
- How does Mr Rabbetts, the head keeper, suspect Danny's father injured his foot?
- Why does the keeper carry a gun?
- Why does Danny break out in a cold sweat?

Predicting
- Will the pheasants all be asleep when Danny and his father return to the wood?
- Will their plan work or will they be discovered?
- Will the keeper remember he saw them and try to accuse them of what has been done?

Main ideas
- Look at how Danny is punished at school and discuss whether physical punishment, such as caning, is fair. Is hitting children a good way to discipline them?

Language, structure and presentation
- In the description of Captain Lancaster, how does Danny/Dahl show his dislike for this character? What words are used?
- What does 'in cold blood' mean?
- What does 'groggy' mean?
- Why does Danny have snakes in his tummy, rather than butterflies? What does this mean?
- What does the word 'pungent' mean?

SESSION 5: A VILLAGE OF POACHERS?

SESSION AIMS

Identify and discuss ideas and themes in part of a book.

BEFORE THE SESSION

The children should have read Chapters 16 and 17 independently before the session.

READ

- Ask the children to remind themselves of what happens in Chapters 16 and 17, while thinking about the following points:
  - The title of Chapter 16 repeats part of the title of the book. What does that tell you about what is happening in this chapter?
  - Examine Danny's descriptions of his father, especially his facial expressions.
- Ask them to read Chapters 18 and 19 independently.

During reading

- Consider Danny's reactions to events and how people behave.
- If your school uses reading journals then the children should be encouraged to make notes as they read and consider each question.
- Move around the group and 'tune in' to hear individuals read aloud. Encourage and praise good expression.

REVISIT AND RESPOND

Use the following discussion points to help the children think about what they have read in more depth.

Note: Since there are only 20 minutes for each session, you are advised to focus on only one or two of the elements that are listed below.

- Chapter 16 has nearly the same title as the book itself, and this is based on the fact that Danny's father calls him 'the champion of the world'. Ask the children why the father feels this way about his

son. Does it seem like an exaggeration to them? Ask: *Does what happens in this chapter match what you thought the book would be about and why Danny is such a champion? Why does Danny deny that he is the champion? Does he not want to be one?* You could have a discussion based on what 'champions' are and what qualities a person needs to be one, and whether Danny meets these requirements or not.

- In Chapter 17, Danny's father and Charlie explain who will help them with the pheasants, and who will also enjoy receiving some, including the local policeman, the doctor and the vicar's wife. Ask: *Why is Danny so shocked at who is helping them with their trick? Are you as shocked as Danny?* Ask them what they think Roald Dahl wants them to think about the situation. Does he present two sides of the story in Danny's reaction (that stealing is bad but that Mr Hazell is a horrible man about to shoot helpless pheasants, so it's not a crime)? How do the children feel about the fact that these pheasants will die anyway, just at the hands of Danny's father and his friends, rather than in the shooting party? Do they agree with Danny's father's opinion that 'We've done these birds a great kindness putting them to sleep…'? What outcome would the children want for the birds?

- In Chapter 18, Danny's father talks about spending their savings money on a cooker and a deep freezer but Danny isn't keen. Ask: *Why is Danny so worried about his father spending money? Shouldn't it be the other way around, with the father worrying and his son wanting to spend money? Why has the author turned the tables here on their relationship?* Ask the children if they think that the money should be spent on something else and, if so, what? Bearing in mind what they know of Danny's mother, if she were still alive do they think she would approve of buying the cooker and the deep freezer? Finally, ask them why Danny's father has never used this money before? Is this fair?

- Ask the children to look at the pages in Chapter 18 that describe Mrs Clipstone's arrival at the filling-station. How does the author build up tension from the moment Danny's father spots her in the

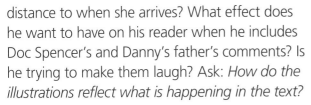

distance to when she arrives? What effect does he want to have on his reader when he includes Doc Spencer's and Danny's father's comments? Is he trying to make them laugh? Ask: *How do the illustrations reflect what is happening in the text?*

- Doc Spencer says that the sleeping pills were wearing off and that was why the pheasants had started trying to escape. Ask: *Do you think Danny's father and the others should have known this? Was this bad planning? Why didn't they kill the birds earlier, or the night before, rather than wait till the next day?* Danny never mentioned this in his planning, so do the children think that he didn't want the birds to die, perhaps?

Ask the children, whenever appropriate, to revisit the text to exemplify/support their answers.

Encourage the children to read aloud to the group when referring back to the text – praise clear, confident and expressive reading.

Before the next session
Ask the children to read Chapter 20.

ASSESSMENT OPPORTUNITIES

The following bank of question prompts provides a quick and easy means of monitoring the children's comprehension skills and understanding of the text. The children's answers to a question must be supported by evidence from the text.

Understanding
- How did Danny and his father leave the wood with the pheasants?
- What is the name of the village policeman?
- How many pheasants did Danny and his father catch?
- What three things should you 'always have' with roasted pheasant?
- What two things does Danny's father want to buy?
- How did Mrs Clipstone deliver the pheasants to the filling-station?

Inferences
- Why is Danny so shocked that the village policeman would take the pheasants?
- Why is Mr Snoddy 'a bit wobbly on his feet'?

- Why was Mrs Clipstone's baby so upset in the pram?
- Why did the lorry driver laugh when a pheasant flew out of the pram?

Predicting
- Will Danny's father be punished for what he has done?
- Will Mr Hazell know that Danny's father is responsible?
- Will they kill all the pheasants?

Language, structure and presentation
- In Chapter 16, the words '*I*' and '*my*' are italicised, as are the words '*deeper*' and '*Thump!*'. Why?
- What does 'doped' mean?
- What does Danny mean when he says 'this poaching lark'?
- What is a 'spit' used for?

Themes and conventions
- Do you think that nasty people get their come-uppance in life as well as in books? Is it all right to act illegally if it is against a nasty person? Is it all right to break the law sometimes?

▼ SESSION 6: IS DANNY THE CHAMPION?

SESSION AIMS

Identify how language, structure and presentation contribute to meaning in a book, particularly in the closing chapters.

BEFORE THE SESSION

The children should have read Chapter 20 independently before the session.

READ

- Ask the children to remind themselves of what happens in Chapter 20, while thinking about the following points:
  - How does Roald Dahl describe Mr Hazell's reaction to the pheasants, particularly his physical appearance?
  - How does Roald Dahl distinguish between the different characters in the chapter, including the way they speak?
- Then ask them to read Chapters 21 and 22 independently.

During reading

- Think about the story as a whole and consider what the future holds for Danny and his father.
- If your school uses reading journals then the children should be encouraged to make notes as they read and consider each question.
- Move around the group and 'tune in' to hear individuals read aloud. Encourage and praise good expression.

REVISIT AND RESPOND

Use the following discussion points to help the children think about what they have read in more depth.

Note: Since there are only 20 minutes for each session, you are advised to focus on only one or two of the elements that are listed below.

- Note some of the similes in Chapter 20 relating to Mr Hazell, and consider what they tell the reader about him. Ask: *Are they funny? Are they intended to make you laugh? What effect does the author want them to have on the reader?* Invite the children to share their favourite simile. Can they think of any other similes of their own for any of the characters in Chapter 20?

- Remind the children that there are quite a few different characters in Chapter 20 and that sometimes, in books, it can be hard for readers to remember the difference between them. Ask: *How does Roald Dahl, in his use of language, differentiate between his characters? Does he do this well?* The children could note down the names of each character mentioned and compare their appearance, how they speak and how others react to them. Which is their favourite character and why?

- In Chapter 20, Danny is shocked that people like the policeman and the vicar's wife are in on the plot. How does the author show this? Do the children know why he might feel this way? (Perhaps because what Danny and his father did was against the law, yet they don't seem to be in trouble for it.) Ask the children what Roald Dahl wants us to believe about a situation where everyone, including the policeman, is going to benefit from an illegal activity such as poaching. Does he agree with it or not? Is this the message that is normally in children's books about stealing? Ask: *Is it ever all right to break the law? If so, in which situations? Does Mr Hazell deserve what has happened to him?*

- Invite the children to think about the final chapter in the book. Ask: *How does the author show how life has changed for Danny and his father since the start of the book? Will life be better for them now? Does the author show a positive future ahead for father and son?* Ask the children to explain their opinions.

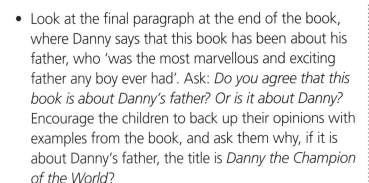

- Look at the final paragraph at the end of the book, where Danny says that this book has been about his father, who 'was the most marvellous and exciting father any boy ever had'. Ask: *Do you agree that this book is about Danny's father? Or is it about Danny?* Encourage the children to back up their opinions with examples from the book, and ask them why, if it is about Danny's father, the title is *Danny the Champion of the World*?

Ask the children, whenever appropriate, to revisit the text to exemplify/support their answers.

Encourage the children to read aloud to the group when referring back to the text – praise clear, confident and expressive reading.

ASSESSMENT OPPORTUNITIES

The following bank of question prompts provides a quick and easy means of monitoring the children's comprehension skills and understanding of the text. The children's answers to a question must be supported by evidence from the text.

Understanding

- What happened to Mr Hazell's car when everyone tried to shoo the pheasants away?
- What will the vicar have for supper instead of pheasant?
- Why did six pheasants never escape?
- Who took the remaining pheasants back to the village, and how?
- What must Danny and his father buy if they have people over for dinner?

Inferences

- Why couldn't Danny repeat what Mr Hazell said to them?
- Why did the pheasants fly in the opposite direction to Hazell Wood?
- Why does Danny admire the policeman and the Doc more than anyone else, apart from his father?

- How will Mr Hazell's guests react to the lack of pheasants?
- Why give your guests the best chairs and cutlery?

Predicting

- Will Danny and his father poach pheasants any more from Mr Hazell?
- Will they succeed at tickling the trout?

Language, structure and presentation

- What does 'resplendent' mean?
- What is a 'rogue'? What is a 'rapscallion'?
- Why does the book finish with the repeated question 'And after that?'? What effect does it have?

GUIDED READING RECORD

Year		Term	
Group		Reading target	

Date	Text	Objectives	Names	Comments

Notes

SCHOLASTIC

READ&RESPOND

Bringing the best books to life in the classroom

BOOK:

....

....

....

....

....

....

....

....

....

....

SCHOLASTIC

READ&RESPOND

Bringing the best books to life in the classroom

BOOK:

....

....

....

....

....

....

....

....

....

....

▼ NOTES

READ & RESPOND

Bringing the best books to life in the classroom

Plan with confidence

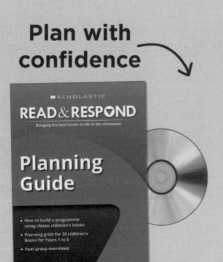

The Planning Guide provides a teaching structure for Years 1–6.

Boost guided reading time

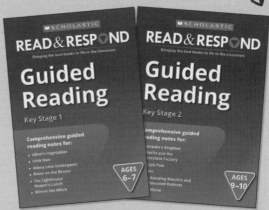

Six guided reading books are available, for Years 1–6.

Teach the best children's books

A huge range of Teacher's Books are available for Years 1–6.

Engage every reader

Children's books are available in sets of 6 and 30.

Order at www.scholastic.co.uk/readandrespond
or call us on 0845 6039091